More POPCORN principles *The Sequel!*

FURTHER CINEMATIC STORYTELLING STRATEGIES FOR NOVELISTS

JOHN GASPARD

ALBERT'S BRIDGE BOOKS

More Popcorn Principles: The Sequel! (Further Cinematic Storytelling Strategies for Novelists)

First Edition | September 2023

https://www.albertsbridgebooks.com

Unless otherwise noted in the Notes section, all quotes are taken from interviews the author conducted for the books "Fast Cheap and Under Control," "Fast Cheap and Written That Way," "Tell Them It's a Dream Sequence," "Women Make Movies," and The Fast, Cheap Movie Thoughts Blog.

CONTENTS

INTRODUCTION

♪♪ *"Tell me more, tell me more…"* ♪♪

That memorable refrain from the song "Summer Nights" in the classic movie *Grease* pretty much encapsulate the response to *The Popcorn Principles.* Much like those inquisitive singers seeking more tales of summer romance, readers clamored for more insights into the intriguing Venn diagram wherein movies and novels intertwine.

Hence this eagerly anticipated next installment, *More Popcorn Principles: The Sequel! (Further Cinematic Storytelling Strategies for Novelists).*

I was thrilled by the overwhelming response from writers after the first book came out. Their hunger for further examples from the silver screen to help guide them on their journey to taking their novels up a notch inspired this new collection of 23 tricks and tips.

I have happily assembled this new assortment of cinematic ideas suitable for your fiction writing needs. From the time-traveling escapades of *Back to the Future* … to the raw intimacy of *sex, lies, and videotape* … the surreal enigma that is *Eraserhead* … and the otherworldly charm of *Twin Peaks*. Throughout this short book, we journey once again through diverse tips and tricks that hold the keys to making your already good novel that much better.

If you've journeyed with us before through *The Popcorn Principles*, you know that dismissing "popcorn movies" as mere trivial entertainment would be a grave mistake. Within the heart of these seemingly effortless confections lies the very secrets of outstanding storytelling—secrets we can eagerly unravel and adapt for the world we create in our novels.

More Popcorn Principles: The Sequel! builds on the foundation laid in the first book. Drawing upon my experiences in both the realms of low-budget feature films and the world of novel writing, I've unearthed twenty-three more Popcorn Principles—each an important nugget of storytelling excellence. These principles offer invaluable insights on how to elevate your craft as a novelist.

You can read the book straight through ... or jump to whatever topic catches your fancy. The book is designed so you can pick it up whenever you need a burst of inspiration ... flip to a random page ... and perhaps find the pearl of wisdom you need to help you move forward.

As you read through each example, I invite you to ask yourselves the same question I offered in the first book: "What's my version of this?"

That is, "How can I adapt this idea to fit my needs ... improve my story ... solve my creative problem?"

To assist in that thought process, I've included questions at the end of each chapter, to help you dig a little deeper into the ideas you've just explored.

And, of course, what would this adventure be without the pleasure of indulging in some movie watching assignments—experiencing the very principles we discuss in action on the silver screen. Every chapter ends with a short viewing list, each designed to help elucidate the ideas of that segment. Or, at the very least, entertain you while you think about what you've read.

So, grab your notebook and a bag of popcorn. Let's dive once more into the world of movies. Together, we will cross the bridge between the screen and the page, discovering the answers you seek on your journey as a novelist.

Welcome to *More Popcorn Principles: The Sequel!*

PRINCIPLE #1

BEGINNING IS HARD

"The scariest moment is always just before you start."
   — *Stephen King*

AH, the elusive art of starting something—especially when that something is as big an undertaking as a novel. If you've ever found yourself staring woefully at a blank page, you're not alone. Beginning something new—and its adjacent fears—is, I think, built into our human DNA.

The thing is, it isn't really just one thing we're afraid of. I think there are at least four fears at work when we face a new project:

- *Fear of the Unknown:* The unfamiliarity of starting something new can be intimidating. We often feel comfortable in our current routines and environments. Venturing into uncharted territory can trigger anxiety and uncertainty.
- *Fear of Failure:* The fear of failure is a powerful deterrent for many people. Starting something new means risking the possibility that it <u>might not</u> succeed. This fear can paralyze you from taking that first step.

- *Fear of Not Being Perfect*: People may hesitate to start something new if they fear they won't be able to meet their own high standards or expectations. The pressure to be perfect from the outset can prevent you from even trying.
- And finally, perhaps the biggest stumbling block when it comes to starting a new creative project, *Fear of Judgment:* The fear of being judged by others. This can be daunting. We worry about what others will think if we fail or if our efforts are not up to par—whatever that means.

Several movies have attempted to dramatize this writer's fear of the blank page: from Nicholas Cage in *Adaptation*, to Melissa McCarthy in *Can You Ever Forgive Me*, to John Turturro in *Barton Fink*, to Jack Nicholson in *The Shining*. Although, to be fair, this last writer did get words on paper. The only issue was, they were the same ten words over and over: "All work and no play makes Jack a dull boy."

Dylan Kidd, writer/director of the movie *Roger Dodger*, defined the struggle and also offered a solution. He said, "The hardest part by far is the beginning. That's the easiest time to get discouraged and give up. The beginning is hard. You're trying to make order out of chaos, and chaos doesn't want to be ordered. If you can just get through that hard part, then I think you'll be rewarded for your perseverance."

Let's take a moment to bask in the wisdom of Dylan's words. The beginning—oh, it can be a nightmare! The blank page stares back at you, daring you to summon words that you'll weave into worlds and characters. It's as if chaos itself resists the call for order, laughing at your attempts to bring clarity to the storm.

But here's the secret sauce that every filmmaker (and writer and creative person) needs to know: Physics and inertia can be our friends!

As Sir Isaac Newton's first law of motion states, an object at rest tends to stay at rest, and an object in motion tends to stay in motion. The key to overcoming the fear of starting is to break the inertia, to nudge that object of creativity into motion.

Just put something—anything—on paper.

It doesn't have to be perfect; in fact, it rarely is. Begin with a single sentence, a fragment of dialogue, or a vivid image that sparks your imagination. Let those initial words be the catalyst that propels you forward. Once you break through the initial resistance, the momentum will carry you onward.

Think of it this way: it's easier to fix something rotten than to come up with something brilliant from scratch. As Steven Spielberg himself has said: "All good ideas start out as bad ideas. That's why it takes so long."

The secret is to just write something. Anything. You can always change it later. As screenwriting guru William Goldman reminds us, "A good writer is not someone who knows how to write, but how to rewrite."

And filmmaker Paul Thomas Anderson agrees that it's not about the writing; it's about the rewriting: "Screenwriting is like ironing. You move forward a little bit and go back and smooth things out."

Another smart way to start is not to worry about the first page, the first paragraph, the first word, but instead to focus on the story in general. Don't lock yourself down to an opening sentence; instead, think about what the story might be. And put that down on paper.

Filmmaker David Lynch (*Eraserhead*), during his time at the Center for Advanced Film Studies, learned many valuable writing tips from his teacher, Frank Daniel, a renowned Czech filmmaker. (Fun fact: Frank was also my screenwriting teacher!)

One terrific lesson Lynch took away from Daniel's teachings

was a simple yet powerful method for structuring a feature film (which you can adopt when you're shaping your own story): "It's a simple thing he taught me," Lynch said. "If you want to make a feature film, you get ideas for 70 scenes. Put them on 3-by-5 cards. As soon as you have 70, you have a feature film."

These index cards became the building blocks of Lynch's creative process, enabling him to visualize the entire film's structure with ease. Without ever having to think about what might be the first word on Page One.

Lynch's use of index cards exemplifies how a practical approach can be an invaluable tool for filmmakers and writers alike. By distilling his ideas onto tangible cards, Lynch gained a clear sense of the narrative's flow and continuity, ensuring that each scene seamlessly fit into the broader vision of his film.

And he was <u>writing</u>—putting words on paper (okay, ideas on index cards). As Newton taught us, once we start moving, we tend to continue moving.

And as for the fears that are holding us back—the fear of the unknown, fear of failure, fear of not being perfect, and fear of judgment—acknowledge them, but don't let them dictate your actions. Accept that the beginning will be hard, but also recognize that the reward for persevering is immense.

And, hey, take comfort in knowing that even the filmmaking and literary greats have wrestled with this very same demon. Mark Twain once quipped, "The secret to getting ahead is getting started."

Add to that the words of prolific novelist Nora Roberts: "You can fix anything but a blank page."

Simple ideas, yet right on point—getting started is your first step toward finishing.

BEYOND THE SCREEN QUESTIONS

- How can I break through the fear of the unknown, like facing a blank page, and start writing by putting something—anything—on paper, just as Dylan Kidd suggests?
- What strategies can I use to overcome the fear of failure and perfectionism, remembering what Steven Spielberg said: "All good ideas start out as bad ideas"?
- How can I adopt David Lynch's index cards method to structure my novel, allowing me to focus on the story in general and avoid fixating on the perfect opening?
- What practical approaches can I use to find momentum in my writing and avoid getting discouraged, considering Sir Isaac Newton's first law of motion that "an object in motion tends to stay in motion"?
- How do I navigate the fear of judgment from others and embrace the messiness of creation, understanding that the journey from chaos to order is a natural part of the process?

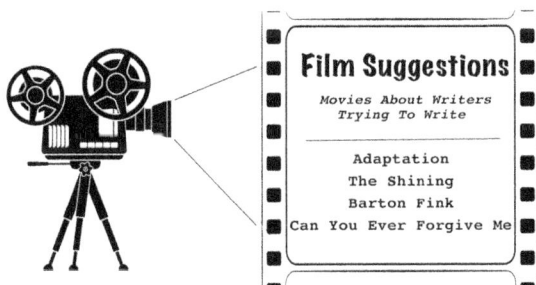

Film Suggestions

Movies About Writers Trying To Write

Adaptation
The Shining
Barton Fink
Can You Ever Forgive Me

PRINCIPLE #2

LISTEN TO THE VOICES IN YOUR HEAD

HERE'S me telling you something you already know: Writing is both an art and a craft.

And while the craft can get you out of trouble when you stumble into it, it's the art that can really take you to places you never imagined you go.

That is, if you allow it to happen.

The key is to let your unconscious into the driver's seat from time to time.

As writer/director Dylan Kidd (*Roger Dodger*) told me, "Your unconscious is trying to tell you what the movie wants to be."

To that end, Kidd allows his unconscious to take over on the first draft of a screenplay, regardless of where it takes him.

Here's how he put it:

"For me, it's really important that the first draft be the spill draft. I'm the exact opposite of someone who knows the ending before they begin. For me, the first draft is the spill-it draft. And after that you can look at it and think, 'Well, I have a 70-page first act, that probably can't work.' For me it's important to follow your bliss in that first draft, even if it ends up at 180 pages or you hate everything but ten percent of it. At least you've got that ten percent, which is ten more than a lot of people have."

Later drafts are when the craft kicks in and you start to edit and hone and tighten and improve. But don't saddle your muse with too many restrictions right out of the gate. Rigidity kills creativity.

Filmmaker and teacher Eric Mendelsohn (*Judy Berlin*) puts it this way: "Here's what I always say to my students: learn a lot, know a lot, then feel a lot.

"You want to feel a lot. You want to be open on the set. You want to be open when you're writing. You want to be open when you're editing. It's a real juggling act of roles that you have to play, of being naive, being smart, being a businessperson, being a general, being a very, very wounded flower.

"I remember reading, as a high school student, Gloria Swanson's autobiography. I remember they asked, 'What are you proudest of in your career.' And she said without hesitation, 'That I'm still vulnerable.'

"And I didn't even know if I understood it at the time, but I get it now.

"You want to be smart. You want to be experienced. But you also want to still be naive and vulnerable. Those are hard things to ask of anyone. But if you want to be in this industry—an art form that so many greats have invested their life's work toiling in—then you owe it to yourself to be all of those things."

There is clearly a delicate balance between the art and craft of writing. The craft serves as a safety net, helping us navigate through rough patches, but it's the art that truly allows our imagination to soar. The key is to let our unconscious mind take the wheel at times, as it can reveal the essence of what our story wants to be.

Dylan Kidd emphasizes the importance of letting the first draft be a "spill-it" draft, even if it leads to unexpected and unconventional outcomes. It's about following our bliss and allowing our creativity to flow freely without being bogged down by constraints from the outset. Subsequent drafts are where the craft comes into play, helping us refine and improve the work.

Eric Mendelsohn advises aspiring writers to learn … know … and then feel deeply. Being open to emotions, experiences, and vulnerabilities is crucial for creative success. He shares the wisdom of Gloria Swanson, who prided herself on remaining vulnerable throughout her career, acknowledging that this balance—of being smart, experienced, yet naive and open—is challenging but essential for those in an artistic industry.

BEYOND THE SCREEN QUESTIONS

- What techniques do you currently use to allow your unconscious mind and creativity to take over during the writing process? How could you improve or expand those techniques?
- How rigid are your outlining and planning processes before you begin writing? Are there ways you could loosen those restrictions to allow for more creative freedom initially?
- Think of your most recent first draft. Did you find yourself following your initial creative impulses, or did you impose constraints that limited your story's potential? What lessons can you take from this?
- In your next writing project, how will you strive for a "spill draft"—a free flowing first draft that follows

your bliss? What obstacles might get in the way, and how can you overcome them?

- What role does vulnerability play in your own creative process? How can you embrace and build on your own vulnerabilities to enhance your writing?

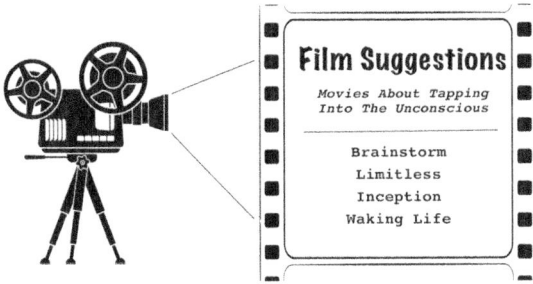

Film Suggestions

Movies About Tapping Into The Unconscious

Brainstorm
Limitless
Inception
Waking Life

PRINCIPLE #3

IGNORE THE VOICES IN YOUR HEAD

OF COURSE, all those voices in your head aren't necessarily trying to help you.

As you write, you may begin to second-guess critics or editors or agents or readers or (worst of all) yourself.

You've got to learn to ignore those voices, because they won't help you write a good novel; they'll just help you destroy your inspiration.

Screenwriter William Goldman put it this way: "Writing is finally about one thing: going into a room alone and doing it. Putting words on paper that have never been there in quite that way before. And although you are physically by yourself, the haunting Demon never leaves you—that Demon being the knowledge of your own terrible limitations, your hopeless inadequacy, the impossibility of ever getting it right."

These negative inner voices can take many forms. A few include:

- *The Imposter Syndrome Voice:* You may feel like you are not truly skilled or talented enough to be considered a "real" writer, attributing your successes to luck rather than your abilities.

- *The Perfectionism Voice:* You may doubt your work's quality, constantly feeling that it is not good enough or polished to be shared with others.
- *The Comparison Voice:* You may constantly compare yourself to other writers, feeling inadequate or inferior in comparison to those you perceive as more successful or accomplished.
- *The Rejection Voice:* You may doubt your work's worthiness and fear rejection or criticism from publishers, agents, or readers.
- *The Self-Censorship Voice:* You may doubt the authenticity or appropriateness of your ideas or writing voice, leading you to self-censor and stifle your creativity.
- *The Fear of Failure Voice:* You may doubt your ability to succeed in the competitive and unpredictable world of publishing, leading you to hesitate or give up on your writing dreams.

You may have one or more of those voices rattling around in your head … or an unhealthy mélange of all of them. Screenwriters and filmmakers grapple with those same voices and many have found coping methods that, at the very least, silence that persistent unhelpful yelping.

Film director Stuart Gordon came out of the cutting-edge Chicago theater scene, and he became accustomed to not worrying about how people—especially critics—would react to his work.

With his first movie, *Re-Animator*, he adopted a similar mindset before he had shot even one frame of his infamous film, which is a cult classic horror film, known for its outrageous and gory scenes, dark humor, and inventive use of mad science. It has gained infamy for pushing the boundaries of horror and its graphic depiction of reanimated corpses and gruesome experiments, making it a standout entry in the genre.

"I just wrote off the critics," Gordon explained. "In a way, that was a very healthy thing, because if you're worrying about the critics, it can paralyze you or you'll get too self-conscious about what you're doing. To just be able to ignore them completely was actually a very healthy thing."

Screenwriter Dan Futterman came to that same realization when he began work on his first script, the Academy Award-nominated screenplay for *Capote*.

Capote is a movie about the famous writer Truman Capote as he investigates a real-life murder case for his book, *In Cold Blood*. During that process, Capote forms an unexpected bond with one of the killers. It's a gripping and intense film that explores the complexities of true crime writing and the impact it has on the author's life.

Futterman told me that, as he worked on the script, he consciously avoided "thinking things like 'How will critics respond to this? How will producers respond to this? How will …?'

"You cannot have that in your head while you're writing," Futterman explained. "You simply have to be thinking, 'Do I like this? Do I believe it? Is it interesting to me? When I go back and read it, if I can be as objective as possible, is it exciting for me to read?'

"If you're honest with yourself and have some sort of decent barometer for how things are playing, then you can't help but have the right reaction to it," Futterman continued. "That's the most important thing, to write something that is successful on the page. That sort of second-guessing, I think, is going to be defeatist. You already have enough voices in your head—and the superego perched on your shoulder, saying, 'That's terrible, that's not good enough'—so the fewer voices you can add to that chorus, the better."

Writers and directors, of course, don't hold the monopoly on self-doubt. Those negative inner voices are going to pop up and annoy any creative person when they begin the process of creating something new.

Actor Jon Hamm had to deal with that negative self-doubt early in his career when he'd go into auditions.

"I kept trying to push down the voice that was saying, 'You're terrible. Someone's better than you,'" Hamm recalled. However, he didn't fall victim to that voice. "I just kept auditioning. I kept showing up and I kept trying."

Even Tom Hanks—that's right, Tom Hanks—has had to grapple with self-doubt and the imposter syndrome.

"No matter what you've done, there comes a point where you think: 'When are they going to discover that I am, in fact, a fraud and take everything away from me?'" he recalled.

"I think that is real to all of us: the stark terror of a loss of confidence in ourselves. No matter who we are, no matter what we've done, there comes a point where you think how did I get here and am I going to be able to continue this? It's a high-wire act that we all walk: I know that at 3 o'clock tomorrow afternoon, I am going to have to deliver some degree of emotional goods. And if I can't do it, that means I'm going to have to fake it. And if I fake it, that means they may catch me at faking it. And if they catch me at faking it, well, then it's just doomsday."

That doomsday feeling is common to all of us. Self-doubt is like an unwanted guest at the creativity party. But we're not alone in dealing with those pesky doubts. Even the greats like

Tom Hanks have their moments of imposter syndrome. The trick is to trust our instincts, ignore the naysayers (even if it's our own inner critic), and just write from the heart.

As Jon Hamm says, "Keep showing up and keep trying!"

BEYOND THE SCREEN QUESTIONS

- Do you recognize any negative inner voices, like the Imposter Syndrome or Fear of Failure, that might be holding you back from writing freely?
- Are you second-guessing yourself too much and worrying about what critics, agents, or readers might think instead of focusing on your own creative vision?
- How can you adopt a mindset like director Stuart Gordon and ignore the critics to write fearlessly and with more freedom?
- Do you tend to overthink and self-censor your ideas? How can you break free from those restrictions and allow your creativity to flow more naturally?
- What can you learn from screenwriter Dan Futterman and trust your instincts, writing what excites and interests you, rather than constantly second-guessing yourself or seeking external approval?

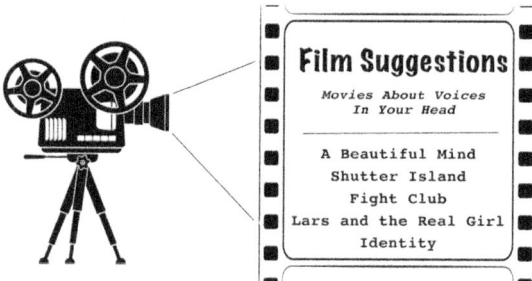

Film Suggestions

Movies About Voices In Your Head

A Beautiful Mind
Shutter Island
Fight Club
Lars and the Real Girl
Identity

PRINCIPLE #4

IGNORE THE VOICES OUTSIDE OF YOUR HEAD

CREATING ANYTHING NEW—A movie, novel, or even a startup company—means venturing into unknown territory. This inevitably brings uncertainty, doubt, and criticism from others.

But great art and innovation arise when creative people can tune out that noise and trust their inner vision.

Here are a couple lessons from filmmakers on how to persist in the face of naysayers.

David Lynch learned the hard way during the making of his breakthrough film *Eraserhead* that what he had created—even though it has since been lionized as a classic—was simply not to everyone's taste.

"We showed it to one guy who was a friend of Terrence Malick, his financial backer, I think," Lynch recalled. "So, we organized several scenes, and this man came in and sat down and I was, you know, trembling. And in the middle of this thing, the man stood up and screamed: 'PEOPLE DON'T ACT LIKE

THAT! PEOPLE DON'T TALK LIKE THAT! THIS IS BULLSHIT!'
And out he went. But, like, really upset.

"So, I thought, 'Man!', you know, 'This is gonna be really
difficult.'"

While you're unlikely to receive such a vociferous reaction to
the first draft of your novel, remember how Lynch reacted to the
first audience response: He simply continued on and made the
movie he wanted to make.

Filmmakers Stefan Avalos and Lance Weiler faced their own
doubts while making their award-winning low-budget fake
documentary, *The Last Broadcast*. But they also had to deal with
the doubts of people around them.

Avalos told me, "We had no shortage of people telling us that
we were going to fail, at whatever point we were at. Right along
the line, from the moment we said we were going to make a
movie until the moment the movie was on HBO. From beginning
to end, people were always saying, 'That won't work.'"

"Throughout the process, we were always told 'No, you can't
do that,'" Weiler added. "We were told, 'No, you can't make a
film on a desktop computer,' 'You're crazy if you think you can
make it for $900,' 'You're crazy if you're not going to take it to
film,' 'There's no way you can show it at festivals that way.' And
we just kept not listening to those people and kept pushing
through as though we were on a mission."

In addition to the satisfaction of successfully finishing and
distributing their movie, they both also had the satisfaction of
proving all those naysayers wrong.

Director/writer Tom Noonan faced similar skepticism when writing the screenplay for his classic low-budget film, *What Happened Was…*

Despite his excitement about the script, Noonan quickly discovered that his enthusiasm was not universally shared.

"Most people who read the script and who are friends of mine, well-known actors who will remain unmentioned, thought the script was stupid," Noonan told me. "Most of the people I really wanted to do it wouldn't do the movie. I'd written it for my wife, who was busy and unavailable, and then I gave it to all these other people who said, 'I like you, but this script is about nothing.'"

However, Noonan had faith in his own writing abilities, which helped him to ignore the naysayers and persevere.

"I'd written scripts for many years before I wrote that script," he said. "And I was a relatively skilled screenwriter. So, when I wrote it, I really tried to not worry about what people traditionally worry about when they write a script. And when I gave it to people, if they didn't like it, fuck 'em, I don't care. I just liked it so much and thought it was so funny and I had so much fun writing it, that I thought that eventually someone is going to get this. And if they don't, I don't care."

When Richard Linklater's classic low-budget feature, *Slacker,* was finished, it was rejected by most major film festivals. But those rejections only fueled Linklater's determination.

"For every film festival it got accepted to," he recalled, "it was turned down by two, by all the major festivals across the board."

Like all filmmakers trying to break into the festival circuit, he received his share of form rejection letters. However, his odd little movie also inspired some respondents to vent their spleen with non-form letters as well.

One producer from New York who had seen the film wrote: "You are living in an entirely different world, especially when it comes to the world of movie audiences. Your film has no potential for a release. It is too long, there is not enough interesting dialogue to give it a special theme. It does not hold up for anything but a quirky TV program."

That sort of letter would be enough to take the wind out of anyone's sails. But that attitude—the honking bray of the naysayer—only strengthened Linklater's resolve.

"At first, I'm a little depressed at the thought of people like him and various festival programmers out there who are no doubt against the film," he wrote in his diary. "I suddenly get a surge of energy at the thought of this growing opposition and vow I will do everything I can humanly do to make this film a success. All future rejections will spur me on even further. I fantasize that anyone who doesn't like the film will ultimately have to answer for their cowardice or incompetence. A large part of me now feels 'You're either with it or against it. And if you're against it, then fuck you, out of the way!'"

The lesson is clear: have faith in your vision and keep creating, no matter the criticism. Start by trusting in your story, even if others don't yet see its worth. Then persevere through the doubt, the many rejections, and tune out the naysayers. Follow the creative pull within and let that be your guide.

The rest will fall into place once you begin.

BEYOND THE FILM QUESTIONS

- Have you received any negative feedback already? How did it make you feel initially?
- How could you shift your perspective to use it as fuel instead of discouragement?
- What strategies can you implement to "tune out the naysayers" and trust in your own writing abilities?

- What small actions can you take today to make progress on your story, regardless of what others think?
- What would your own version of Linklater's mantra be: 'You're either with it or against it, and if you're against it, then fuck you, out of the way!'?

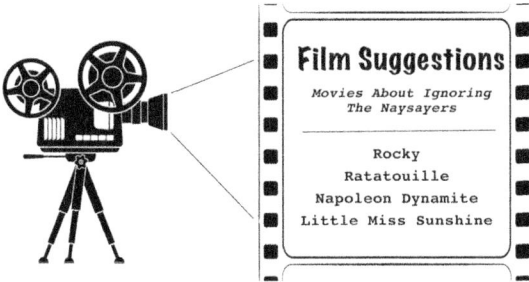

Film Suggestions

Movies About Ignoring The Naysayers

Rocky
Ratatouille
Napoleon Dynamite
Little Miss Sunshine

PRINCIPLE #5

UNRAVELING THE THREAD OF THEME

A THEME IS a great thing to have.

Some writers begin their story with their theme clearly in mind. Others don't discover it until they are well on their way. And a few don't recognize the theme until well after they've typed "The End."

But once you know what it is, a theme can provide a great touchstone to return to, any time you get lost or are unsure where to head next, story-wise.

Themes are just as important to screenwriters and filmmakers.

To help us better understand how a theme can shape a narrative, let's explore the perspectives of filmmakers Ron Howard, Darren Aronofsky, Henry Jaglom, and Eric Bogosian. They will shed light on the significance of theme in the creation of their movies, *Grand Theft Auto*, *Pi*, *Someone to Love*, and *subUrbia*, respectively.

Ron Howard, the star, co-writer and director of the Roger Corman car chase classic, *Grand Theft Auto*, emphasized the importance of establishing a theme early on in the screenwriting process.

Grand Theft Auto is a fast-paced, action-packed comedy film, centered around a young couple who embark on a wild and reckless cross-country chase to save their relationship.

Despite the movie's comedic nature, Howard and his co-writer (his father, Rance Howard) took the story seriously and sought to infuse it with a thematic center.

"No matter how silly a movie might be," Ron Howard said, "I've always felt it has to have a point of view, and it has to have a thematic center. Those themes may not be very complex, but they do have to be well thought out. My dad and I, when we were working on the script, we did see it as a kind of a parable about the power of love."

Establishing that theme early on can help enormously during production, when a director is barraged with thousands of questions and often must make quick decisions.

"So much of directing is managing your compromises," Ron Howard agreed. "And making these quick, knee-jerk decisions can have minor significance on a shot-by-shot basis. But over the course of the entire picture, it numbers in the thousands. And if they are informed or at least fueled by some sort of thematic objective—even if you're having to cut something out or change something on the fly—you're keeping the big ideas in place. And it helps make those decisions more cohesive."

As a novelist, you're making thousands of decisions during your writing process. With the story's theme sharply defined in your head, you'll always have a stronger and clearer sense of which turn to take any time you're faced with a decision.

In contrast to *Grand Theft Auto*, Darren Aronofsky's *pi* demonstrated a highly stylized approach to storytelling.

Pi is a mind-bending, highly stylized psychological thriller, following a brilliant mathematician who becomes obsessed with uncovering the hidden patterns of nature and the stock market, leading him into a dangerous spiral of paranoia and discovery. However, Aronofsky emphasized that the film's stylization served the purpose of enhancing the narrative rather than being stylistic for its own sake.

"You start with your theme and your story," Aronofsky explained. "Whenever you know what your theme is and what your theme is about, there's only one place to put the camera. There is only one place that you tell the story from. The film is very clear once you understand that. That's what I search for when I go onto a set: what angle is going to really tell this. Then I have every department approach it that way."

Knowing his theme ahead of time helped make every decision on the film—from every department—consistent and congruent with his vision. Although he followed this approach on *pi*, Aronofsky was surprised to learn something about his theme while in the midst of making his movie.

"While working on this movie on paranoia," he recalled, "I started to realize that the filmmaking process is a paranoid experience. Because they always tell you in filmmaking that every single scene should relate to your main character, relate to your theme. And that's exactly what paranoid schizophrenics think their world is: That the entire world relates to them. So, filmmaking is a paranoid experience."

The idea of living in an imaginary world (which you are creating with your words) highlights the importance of having a solid grasp of your story's theme. Without a well-thought-out theme, you'll risk feeling lost and lacking clarity at key points in your narrative.

Henry Jaglom's approach to his highly personal film, *Someone to Love*, differed significantly from traditional filmmaking methodologies.

Someone to Love is a whimsical and introspective film revolving around a group of Hollywood actors who come together on Valentine's Day to confront their loneliness and explore the complexities of love and relationships in a heartfelt and comedic journey.

Instead of meticulously planning and scripting, Jaglom allowed the theme of loneliness to guide his entire creative process. "I had a plan, a super structure," Jaglom explained. "I knew what I wanted to talk about in terms of loneliness and relationships, but I was actually seeking the movie as I was in the movie. I decided I would just do it that way and then when I got back to my editing room, I would look at what everybody gave me and find a way to put it together into a narrative.

"I didn't set out to work this way," he added. "It's the way I like finding stories."

This approach—letting the theme drive the train and finding the story only once you get into the edit—is for Jaglom a risky but ultimately rewarding way to work.

"Orson Welles always said that the difference between me and other filmmakers, was other filmmakers write their film and while they're writing it, they try to find their theme," Jaglom recounted. But that isn't how he creates. "I decide on my theme and hammer away at the theme until I get the story. The story is always very secondary to me."

That's a completely legitimate way to work: Start with the theme and then find the story by exploring that theme from various angles. Much the same can be said of our next screenwriter, Eric Bogosian.

Eric Bogosian, whose play *subUrbia* was adapted into a film by Richard Linklater, demonstrates the significance of theme as a foundational element in his writing process.

The play and movie delve into the lives of restless young adults who gather in a convenience store parking lot, confronting their dreams, frustrations, and the uncertainties of their futures while grappling with the consequences of their choices.

"I always begin with a theme," Bogosian told me. "I begin with character and theme. The theme dances around in my head, almost like an editing device as I put my characters in motion with a story. But before anything, I think of the people who will populate my stage. In the case of *subUrbia*, I began with five student actors in a workshop playing the characters. I had them simply hanging out and discussing a variety of topics. There was no plot to speak of in the first set of pages."

Working this way allows the characters to form themselves right in front of his eyes. "The characters are there within me," Bogosian explained. "They are the archetypes I 'need' to conceptualize my inner world. In the case of *subUrbia*, the cast of characters derived almost directly from the cast of characters who, in my mind, represent my friends from my high school days."

Just as he did with *SubUrbia*, Bogosian would never start a project without first landing on its theme.

"I always begin with a theme. It usually morphs as I'm writing, but in the long run, the theme must have importance for me in the present, as I'm writing. I need the theme to do my writing, but I don't mind if the audience doesn't see the theme or misunderstands what the theme is."

So, think about how these four filmmakers utilized themes in their work and ask yourself, what's my version of that?

Ron Howard's emphasis on establishing a theme early in the screenwriting process provides a strong foundation for decision-making during production.

Darren Aronofsky's approach of letting the theme guide every step of the process highlights how your theme can provide clarity and purpose.

Henry Jaglom's unconventional method of allowing the theme to lead the creative process demonstrates the potential rewards of exploring themes from various angles.

Similarly, Eric Bogosian's emphasis on starting with a theme and letting it evolve throughout the writing process emphasizes the significance of themes as foundational elements in story-telling.

A story's theme can be elusive yet critically important. Stay open as your characters develop—they may reveal themes you hadn't considered. And remember, your ultimate goal isn't to prove a theme, but to use your theme to explore what it means to be human.

BEYOND THE SCREEN QUESTIONS

- Have you established a clear and meaningful theme for your story before or during the writing process to serve as a touchstone for decision-making?
- How can you let the theme guide every step of the creative process to ensure consistency and purpose in your narrative?
- Are you open to unconventional methods of storytelling, like Henry Jaglom, where the theme drives the train, and the story emerges through exploration?

- Do you have a strong grasp of your characters and their relationships to the theme, allowing them to form naturally and authentically?
- Is your theme personally significant to you as the writer, even if it may not be overtly apparent to the audience? How can you use it as a driving force to enhance your storytelling?

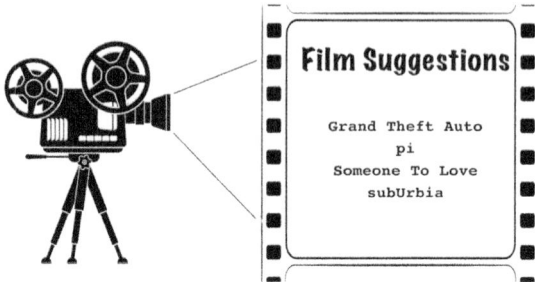

Film Suggestions

Grand Theft Auto
pi
Someone To Love
subUrbia

PRINCIPLE #6
RAISE THE STAKES

"You have to get your hero up a tree and then once he's up there, throw rocks at him."

AS FAR AS I can tell, this quote dates back at least as far as the late 1800s, offering solid advice about how to create an engaging dramatic piece: Make things as difficult as possible for your hero.

In Hollywood, it's been shortened to three simple words: "Raise the stakes." In fact, those words are probably the most repeated phrase at development meetings throughout the greater Los Angeles area. Right next to, "What's for lunch?"

So, what does it mean in concrete terms to raise the stakes?

For me, it's best encapsulated by a couple utterances from the character of scientist Walter Kornbluth (Eugene Levy) in the classic mermaid comedy, *Splash*.

Throughout the story, Kornbluth says on more than one occasion, "What a week I'm having!"

That's raising the stakes in a nutshell: things need to go from bad to worse.

For a more extreme example, check out the BBC series, *Worst Week of My Life*, which is a near perfect (if exaggerated) example of how to raise the stakes on your main character by getting him up into a tree. And then throwing rocks at him. Again and again and again.

There are, of course many kinds of stakes you can raise. Here are five possible approaches, along with some representative examples:

Increase the Personal Cost: Make sure there is something personally at stake for your hero.

In the movie *Casablanca*, Rick Blaine must make a challenging decision when his former lover, Ilsa Lund, reappears in his life. As World War II rages around them, Ilsa seeks Rick's help to escape Casablanca with her resistance leader husband, Victor Laszlo. Rick's personal cost comes in the form of sacrificing his love for Ilsa and aiding her and Victor's escape, putting his own safety at risk in the process.

In *The Dark Knight*, Batman's alter ego, Bruce Wayne, faces the dilemma of having to choose between saving his love interest, Rachel Dawes, or Harvey Dent, Gotham City's District Attorney, both of whom are held captive by the Joker. Bruce Wayne's decision has a profound personal cost as he is forced to make a choice that will change the course of his life and relationships forever.

Introduce a Ticking Clock: Increase the tension by adding a tightening element to the hero's predicament.

High Noon centers on Marshal Will Kane, who is set to retire and leave town with his new wife. However, he receives news that a criminal he once put away is arriving on the noon train to seek revenge. Kane has a ticking clock counting down to a high noon showdown with the vengeful outlaw, creating suspense and tension throughout the film—made all the more dramatic because the story takes place in real time.

In *Speed*, a bomb is planted on a city bus, and if the bus drops below 50 miles per hour, the bomb will explode, killing everyone onboard. The protagonist, LAPD officer Jack Traven, must keep the bus moving at that speed while also trying to find a way to safely evacuate the passengers. The ticking clock of the bus's speed adds constant tension and urgency to the film.

Make the Antagonist Formidable: Audiences will worry more about the hero if the opponent really seems unbeatable.

In *The Silence of the Lambs*, Clarice Starling, an FBI trainee, seeks the help of the incarcerated and brilliant serial killer, Dr. Hannibal Lecter, to catch another serial killer, Buffalo Bill. Lecter is a formidable and manipulative antagonist, constantly challenging and testing Clarice's wits as she tries to outmaneuver him.

In *No Country for Old Men*, the antagonist, Anton Chigurh, is a deeply formidable hitman. His relentless pursuit of stolen money and his unconventional moral code, symbolized by his repeated coin tosses, makes him an enigmatic and terrifying force.

Put the Main Character's Values to the Test: Put your hero in a position where they are challenged to defend (or change) their core beliefs.

In *Schindler's List*, the main character, Oskar Schindler, is a German businessman who initially exploits Jewish labor during World War II to profit from the war economy. However, as he witnesses the horrors of the Holocaust and the systematic extermination of Jews, his values and conscience are profoundly challenged.

In *On the Waterfront*, Terry Malloy is a former prizefighter who works for a corrupt union boss. As he witnesses the corruption and abuse of power, Terry must decide whether to remain silent and continue to be complicit, or stand up against the union and its brutal tactics, risking his life and relationships.

Escalate the Threat to the World: Put your hero in a situation that could literally result in the end of the world.

In the black comedy, *Dr. Strangelove: Or, How I Learned to Stop Worrying and Love the Bomb*, the world faces the escalating threat of nuclear war as a deranged U.S. Air Force general orders a nuclear strike on the Soviet Union without proper authorization. The film satirizes the tension and paranoia of the Cold War era, while the potential consequences of global destruction raise the stakes to an absurdly high level.

In contrast to the darkly comedic satire of *Dr. Strangelove*, *Fail-Safe* presents a more serious and intense examination of the escalating threat to the world during the Cold War. While both films revolve around the dangers of nuclear war, *Dr. Strangelove* uses dark humor to highlight the absurdity and incompetence of those in power, whereas *Fail-Safe* takes a somber and thought-provoking approach.

Study the different approaches outlined above and ask yourself, "What's my version of that?"

Screenwriter Kelly Masterson learned firsthand the value of raising the stakes for his characters in his first produced screenplay, *Before the Devil Knows You're Dead*. I asked him what was going on in his writing career before he started work on that script.

"Nothing," Masterson told me. "My career was dead in the water. I was working at a bank in Manhattan. The script was optioned by a succession of producers but I had lost hope after several false starts."

That all changed when he got a call out of the blue from the producers, telling him that the project was a go.

"They had Sidney Lumet on board to direct," Masterson recounted. "The entire cast was in place: Philip Seymour Hoffman, Albert Finney, Ethan Hawke and Marisa Tomei. I was totally shocked. I got that call on May 16th and they started shooting on July 10. I had no time to react. I quit my job at the bank as soon as the money cleared."

I asked him what it was about that script that had made the difference and inspired so many high-profile creatives to jump on board. He said the answer was simple: he had raised the stakes.

"I dug deeper," Masterson explained. "I made things more personal and more emotionally significant (for the characters). While I often try to pull my characters in two or more directions, I think Sidney's contribution took my material into richer psychological territory. This gave the wonderful actors great stuff to work with in which the emotional stakes were very high.

"When I am working on projects now, I ask myself the question: how do I get further into this character and really rock him?"

Screenwriting guru Robert McKee agrees: "True character is revealed in the choices a human being makes under pressure—the greater the pressure, the deeper the revelation, the truer the choice is to the character's essential nature."

While we may understand this on an intellectual level, it is often difficult to take a character we love and be the one to make terrible things happen to them.

If that's what's holding you back, I'll leave you with the words of writer Kurt Vonnegut, who offered the following permission:

"Be a sadist. No matter how sweet and innocent your leading characters, make awful things happen to them—in order that the reader may see what they are made of."

BEYOND THE SCREEN QUESTIONS

- What personal goals, desires, or relationships are at stake for your main character?

- How can you introduce a ticking clock or time-sensitive element to increase tension and urgency in the story?
- Is your antagonist compelling and formidable enough to challenge the protagonist?
- What core beliefs and values drive your main character's actions, and how can you put them to the test?
- Are there unforeseen consequences or moral dilemmas that you can introduce to add complexity and intensity to the narrative?

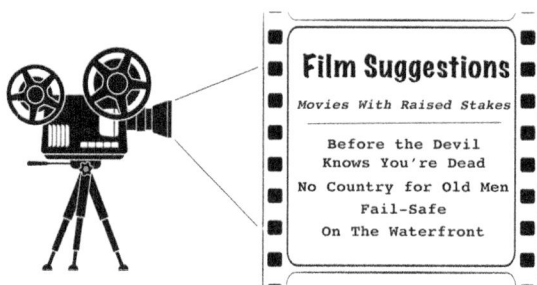

Film Suggestions

Movies With Raised Stakes

Before the Devil
Knows You're Dead
No Country for Old Men
Fail-Safe
On The Waterfront

PRINCIPLE #7
TAKE BIG SWINGS

SOMETIMES YOU JUST HAVE TO SWING FOR the fences.

If you're looking for permission, here it is: If you've got a different idea, a new approach or a radical vision, give it a shot.

Take that big swing.

Filmmaker Tom DiCillo learned not to be afraid to take big swings on his classic low-budget feature, *Living in Oblivion*. Many of the things he did on that movie—like switching from black and white to color during the course of the film … or breaking the movie into three separate but inter-related shorts— might have been dismissed out of hand by some filmmakers. But he didn't let that stop him. He just took a big swing.

As DiCillo put it: "Whatever you're doing, if you're trying something, just try it. Things don't have to be instantaneously perfect or whatever. But if you really are trying something, then trust it and just try it."

Several filmmakers have ignored conventional wisdom and proven that it occasionally pays off to take big swings:

- At the time of its release, Stanley Kubrick's sci-fi masterpiece *2001: A Space Odyssey* defied the conventions of traditional narrative storytelling. The film is known for its enigmatic and abstract visuals, minimal dialogue, and its willingness to leave much of the story open to interpretation.
- Spike Jonze's *Being John Malkovich* is a mind-bending and original film that explores identity and celebrity culture. Spike Jonze, along with writer Charlie Kaufman, took a bizarre premise of a portal into the mind of actor John Malkovich and turned it into a darkly comedic exploration of human desires and aspirations.
- Richard Linklater's *Boyhood* is an ambitious project that takes place over twelve years, following the life of a boy as he grows into adolescence. Linklater defied the traditional filmmaking process by shooting the film in short segments over the course of those years, using the same cast as they aged naturally.

Filmmaker Roger Nygard moves easily between documentaries (*Trekkies*), features (*Suckers*) and directing and editing television shows (*The Office, Curb Your Enthusiasm*). His low-budget feature, *Suckers*, examines the workings of a car dealership, following the salespeople as they do everything in their power to reach their sales goals.

The big swing that Nygard employed on that film was creating a unique storytelling structure: The scenes in the film take place on four consecutive Saturdays. Nothing is shown outside of those four days.

When I asked Nygard why he adopted the story structure he did, he explained: "That was because that's how the car business runs. Every Saturday there's a sales meeting. It's an inspirational meeting, a motivational meeting. It's a time for everybody to gauge where they are against everyone else, because there's always that competitive aspect. So that's how we broke it down, because the industry that we were writing about breaks itself down monthly and weekly."

(We'll take a deeper dive into alternate story structures in Principle #15 - Play With Structure)

In addition to that odd story structure, Nygard also took another big swing by setting the entire first act of his film in the sales meeting which kicks off the month of Saturdays.

"You know, we broke a lot of structural rules with *Suckers*," Nygard admitted. "And, in hindsight, there is a lot I would do differently, having learned what I've learned since then. And having seen how that experiment worked, where it worked and where it failed. Part of the excitement of filmmaking is taking chances. Sometimes you're going to fail spectacularly."

That's correct. For every *2001: A Space Odyssey* there is a *Waterworld*.

And for every *Being John Malkovich* there is a *Heaven's Gate*.

Big swings don't always produce home runs.

But taking risks in the world of novel writing doesn't have the financial risks that movies do. We can take more chances. And the results can be spectacular: Neil Gaiman's *American Gods*. James Joyce's *Ulysses*. Kurt Vonnegut's *Slaughterhouse-Five*. Margaret Atwood's *The Handmaid's Tale*. Toni Morrison's *Beloved*. David Foster Wallace's *Infinite Jest*.

As a novelist, you have the power to defy conventional wisdom and unleash your creativity. Just like the filmmakers mentioned above took bold risks and found success with their innovative works, you too can take big swings in your writing.

In the world of novels, big swings can lead to spectacular results, and your unique voice and vision may just be the spark that sets your writing apart and resonates with readers worldwide.

BEYOND THE SCREEN QUESTIONS

- Reflect on a unique idea or unconventional approach you've considered for your novel. How might it add depth or intrigue to your story?
- Think about a narrative structure you've never tried before. How could experimenting with it enhance your storytelling?
- Imagine taking a "big swing" like the filmmakers mentioned in the chapter. What risks would you be willing to take to push the boundaries of your writing? What's your version of that?
- Consider any recurring themes or topics in your novel. How could you approach them from a fresh and unexpected perspective?
- Identify a genre or style you haven't explored yet. How might stepping outside your comfort zone spark new creativity and enrich your writing?

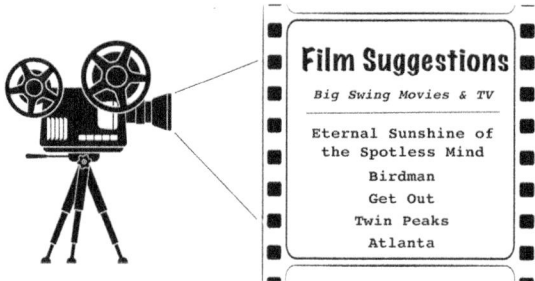

Film Suggestions

Big Swing Movies & TV

Eternal Sunshine of the Spotless Mind

Birdman

Get Out

Twin Peaks

Atlanta

PRINCIPLE #8
ARE YOU REPEATING YOURSELF?

IN THE BEST SCREENPLAYS, if something is repeated, it's repeated for a reason.

The tight structure of a well-made script simply doesn't leave any room for unnecessary repetitions. And any unnecessary repetitions which make it into the production schedule, and are filmed, will likely be removed at some point in the editing process.

The dramatic reasoning is solid: if a character says or does the same thing twice, it should be for a distinctive reason. If not, it has to go.

The same should be true in our novels. When an action or a line of dialogue is repeated, it needs to be for dramatic effect … and not because we forgot that we already used it before.

For filmmaker Rebecca Miller (*Personal Velocity*), this is an important step in her writing process. She recommends that we "comb through [the script] for repetitions. If you say the same thing two different ways, usually you don't need to do that. It's a very powerful medium."

Which means that when we have a character say or do the same thing twice, it better have some dramatic value. Remember Dr. Kornbluth in *Splash*, repeating the phrase "What a week I'm having!" Movies offer many memorable examples of well-placed repetitions:

In *The Godfather*, Don Vito Corleone says "I'm gonna make him an offer he can't refuse." Later in the film when his son Michael uses the same phrase, we understand the drastic change in values Michael has undergone over the course of the film.

Rick's classic line "Here's looking at you, kid" in *Casablanca*, encapsulates the bittersweet past and his enduring love of Ilsa, making it a poignant and memorable motif in the story. The first time he says it, we know he's in love. The second time, we know his heart is broken.

In *Butch Cassidy and The Sundance Kid*, Butch's repeated question about The Super Posse which is following them ("Who are those guys?"), along with the way he says it, demonstrates his growing unease at their situation.

Similarly, the line "Hello, my name is Inigo Montoya. You killed my father. Prepare to die." in *The Princess Bride* becomes far more meaningful the last time an injured Montoya gasps the words before killing the Six-Fingered Man. Primarily because of how many times he had already uttered that phrase in preparation.

It's not always just about words; even a simple sound can create emotional resonance when it's artfully repeated. In *Once Upon a Time In Hollywood*, early in the film, Brad Pitt gives his dog a command, just by clicking his tongue. Hearing that sound, the dog knows he now has permission to eat his dinner. Pitt makes the same sound in the climax of the film, resulting in a different and more deadly response from the dog.

From a more macro viewpoint, there are several films which are all about repetition:

In the German thriller, *Run, Lola, Run*, the heroine has twenty minutes to save her boyfriend from a dangerous situation. The film presents three separate scenarios, each starting with the same moment and repeating Lola's desperate run with slight variations, leading to drastically different outcomes.

In *It's a Wonderful Life*, George Bailey experiences an alternate reality where he was never born. Throughout the film, specific events and interactions are shown twice: once in the real world and then again in the altered reality, demonstrating the profound impact George has had on the lives of those around him.

Memento follows a character who suffers from anterograde amnesia, meaning he can't form any new memories since the onset of his amnesia. The film uses reverse chronology, repeating scenes from different perspectives. This repetition intensifies the viewer's understanding of the protagonist's mental state and raises questions about the reliability of memory and the search for truth.

And, of course, the film *Groundhog Day* uses repeated actions and dialogue to great effect, to demonstrate how Bill Murray's character changes as he experiences the same day over and over and over. (Someone with way too much time on their hands calculated that Murray repeats the same day 12,395 times over the course of the story.)

It all comes down to intentionality: unintended repetitions will make your writing seem sloppy and drag your story down; well-placed repetitions will increase the depth of your story and demonstrate how your character changes and grows through the course of their journey.

BEYOND THE SCREEN QUESTIONS

- Reflect on your current work in progress: Are there any instances where you find yourself unintentionally repeating actions or lines of dialogue?
- How can you identify these repetitions and ensure they serve a purpose in the narrative?
- Think about the pivotal moments in your story: Are there any key lines or actions that can be repeated later in the plot for added dramatic effect?

- How can these repetitions highlight character growth or changes in values?
- Consider the relationships between your characters: Are there any phrases or gestures that can be used as motifs, evolving and growing in meaning as the story progresses?

Film Suggestions

Watch These More Than Once

Eternal Sunshine of
the Spotless Mind
Inception
Mulholland Drice
The Big Lebowski
The Usual Suspects

PRINCIPLE #9

GET TO THE POINT! AND THEN
LEAVE WHEN IT'S OVER.

WHICH OF US hasn't had this experience: A friend recommends a TV series to you, with the caveat "It starts slow, but it really begins to get interesting about the third or fourth episode."

Really? It's not interesting until the third episode? Then why don't I just start at Episode Three and save some time?

Sadly, the same is true of many novels: They may be terrific once you get into them, but it takes a lot of time—often too much time—for that engine to get up-to-speed. And many readers just aren't that patient. They'll give up on your book long before it's over and—more damaging—they'll tell others not to bother reading it as well.

In *The Popcorn Principles*, we talked about the importance of getting into a scene as late as possible and leaving as early as possible *(Principle #6: Come In Late, Leave Early)*. The same is true with the beginning of your story … and the end of your story.

In Hollywood, the rule of thumb for screenwriters is that you have about three to five pages before a studio reader will bail on a script. If the writer hasn't grabbed them right away—with something interesting and provocative—they will simply set that script aside and reach for the next screenplay on their pile. And there is <u>always</u> another script on their pile. The pile never ends.

Our friend, filmmaker and editor Roger Nygard (*Suckers, Trekkies, Veep, Curb Your Enthusiasm*), looks at it this way: "We don't need all this preamble at the beginning. Let's get right to the conflict, right to the problem, right to the argument, right to the dead body, the infection, the insurrection, whatever."

Look at *Sunset Boulevard*. First scene. Dead body in the pool. Boom. We're in.

The same can be said of *Vertigo*.

Up.

Scream.

Goodfellas.

Jaws.

Wargames.

All very different movies, but they share one key component: They grab the audience in the first scene.

Conversely, when the story is over, get out. Don't dawdle. Don't hang around for another fifty pages. Or, in the case of movies, another twenty minutes (I'm looking at you, *The Lord of the Rings: The Return of the King*.)

Once again, Roger Nygard succinctly explains how it works in the best movies: "Once the bad guy is vanquished, the movie is over. Obviously, you can't go on past that or you've lost the audience. They know when a movie is over."

(This seems like a good time to hype Roger's terrific book, *Cut To The Monkey: A Hollywood Editor's Behind-the-Scenes Secrets to Making Hit Comedies*. The book is the story of a filmmaker's journey through Hollywood—revealing the techniques behind how the experts find the funny in any project—by a filmmaker who has worked with some of the funniest people in the business. I highly recommend it.)

Anyway, the art of simply ending a movie when it's actually over seems to have become a lost art. But there are some movies that knew enough to slap "The End" on the screen at the moment the story was over:

Casablanca

Rocky

The Bridge on The River Kwai

Raiders of the Lost Arc

Star Wars (Episode IV: A New Hope)

Halloween

The movies mentioned above demonstrate that getting right to the action in the opening scenes and wrapping things up the moment the problem is solved makes for an enjoyable tale. Editor Roger Nygard's advice keeps it simple: cut out all the fluff at the beginning, just show us the conflict. And finish the story as soon as the character gets what they want.

When you don't waste time at the start or end, what you're left with is an entertaining yarn that respect's the readers' attention span ... and leaves 'em wanting more.

BEYOND THE SCREEN QUESTIONS

- How quickly does your story get to the main conflict or problem in the opening chapters? Could you cut any extraneous scenes or details at the start and dive right into the action?
- Are there any moments in the first few pages that could hook readers and compel them to keep turning pages? If not, what could you add or change?
- Does your climax arrive naturally as a result of the plot and character arcs, or does it feel too stretched out or abrupt? How could you tighten it up?

- Once the protagonist achieves their goal, does the story remain interesting for much longer? If so, could you end it more decisively at that moment of victory?
- After finishing a full draft, do you do a "merciless editing" pass to cut anything that doesn't propel the plot or develop the characters in an essential way? This may mean shortening both the beginning <u>and</u> the ending.

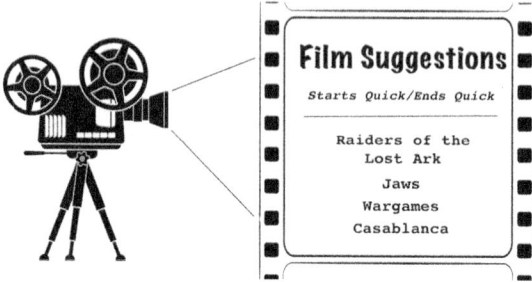

Film Suggestions

Starts Quick/Ends Quick

Raiders of the
Lost Ark

Jaws

Wargames

Casablanca

PRINCIPLE #10
CLIFFHANGERS (GOOD)

CLIFFHANGER ENDINGS CAN BE FRUSTRATING for readers who are looking for a satisfying conclusion to the story. While leaving some questions unanswered can motivate readers to pick up the next installment, an abrupt or undetailed ending can leave readers feeling cheated.

And readers who feel cheated are unlikely to pick up your next book.

Not so surprisingly, I think the answer—that correct balance—can be found in the world of film.

The popular movie, *Back to the Future (Part One)* provides a useful lesson on how to craft a truly satisfying standalone ending, while also setting the stage for further adventures. In other words, how to build a cliffhanger ending that entices but doesn't annoy.

The makers of the first *Back to the Future* film made the wise decision to resolve Marty's central journey and provide complete closure at the end of the first installment. (Probably because at the time they didn't know there would be a second installment; the movie's success was something of a surprise.)

Consequently, viewers were treated to a well-rounded story

with a beginning, middle and end that stands on its own as a classic.

From the beginning, the plot established a clear goal for Marty: to reunite his parents and ensure his own existence. The finale provides emotional closure by reaffirming Marty's relationships with both his parents. Loose ends are tied up and questions answered, giving viewers a clear sense that Marty's story has come full circle: Marty began the movie as an unemployed teenager with little direction. He ends it as a more confident young man with a clearer understanding of his purpose.

Marty's character arc has been fulfilled, the central conflict has been resolved and the film's central premise of time travel has been explored thoroughly.

Yet the film also hints at the possibility of more adventures to come, without resorting to an overt cliffhanger which provides no closure. Doc Brown appears from the future with a dire warning about Marty's kids and the pair once again jump into the souped-up DeLorean ("Roads? Where we're going, we don't need roads.") and they're gone.

Marty and Doc Brown are left in a place where further time travel stories naturally grow from their experiences in the first film, while still providing a satisfying conclusion to this initial adventure.

This highlights an important balance in storytelling. Readers want an ending that feels complete and conclusive, resolving major arcs and questions while providing emotional satisfaction. But a hint of open-endedness can also motivate readers to embark on a new journey with beloved characters, if the sequel is executed skillfully.

Another film with a good cliffhanger ending is *The Three Musketeers* (the 1973 version). At the end of the first of two films,

D'Artagnan has achieved his goal to become a Musketeer. He's established a relationship with Constance, and he has formed an alliance with Athos, Aramis, and Porthos.

Emotionally, the film is over. But at the conclusion, as our heroes literally ride off into the sunset, we see some quick shots of the adventures to come in the sequel, *The Four Musketeers*. Hints are given of what lies ahead for our heroes. As an audience, our emotional arc is complete, and the images entice us to look forward to the next adventure.

(An intriguing sidenote: The 1973 movies *The Three Musketeers* and its sequel *The Four Musketeers,* were shot simultaneously as one production. It was decided in editing to split it into two movies and release them six months apart. This tactic pleased the profit-focused producers, but annoyed the actors, as they had only been paid to make one movie.)

The Three Musketeers and *Back to the Future (Part One)* illustrate how a truly satisfying cliffhanger ending—one that resolves the central conflict, completes a character arc and answers major questions—allows readers to close one chapter fully before opening a new one.

BEYOND THE SCREEN QUESTIONS

- Does your current ending satisfy readers by resolving the central conflict and your protagonist's arc? If not, how could you strengthen the conclusion?
- What major questions do you need to answer to provide a sense of closure for readers at the end of your book? Make a list and ensure they are addressed.
- Does your current ending hint at the potential for future books without resorting to an abrupt cliffhanger? If not, how could you give your story a more *Back to the Future-esque* close?

- If you plan to write a sequel, what foreshadowing or hints could you drop at the end of this book to entice readers, without overly committing to specific plot points?
- How has analyzing the endings of *Back to the Future* and *The Three Musketeers* caused you to rethink or strengthen your own ending? What specific revisions will you make based on these lessons?

Film Suggestions

Good Cliffhanger Endings

Back to the Future
The Three Musketeers
Blade Runner
The Italian Job (1969)
The Thing (1982)

PRINCIPLE #11
CLIFFHANGERS (BAD)

AS MENTIONED in the previous chapter, the use of cliffhangers can be effective tools for serial storytelling, but only if used judiciously.

When done poorly, bad cliffhangers frustrate audiences by leaving major plot threads or character arcs unresolved. However, once you understand what makes bad cliffhangers irritating, you have the tools you need to fix your problematic ending.

Back to the Future Part II and *The Empire Strikes Back* provide chilling examples of cliffhangers which initially upset audiences but were later rectified by satisfying conclusions in their following installments. However, that doesn't change the fact that audiences hated the endings.

For example, when I saw *Back to the Future Part II* in the theater (yes, I'm that old), audience members screamed catcalls at the screen when we were left hanging at the end of the movie. How was Marty going to get out of 1955? How could he save Doc Brown in 1855? Why have you left us hanging?

Audiences had similar responses to the ending of *The Empire Strikes Back* (even though I still think it's the best of the three original films). While George Lucas was basing the ending on those found in the movie serials of the 1930s and 1940s (in which the hero would literally be left hanging from a cliff at the end of the installment), modern moviegoers weren't keen on that approach.

The endings of both films (and any bad cliffhanger) share some common flaws:

- **Unanswered Questions**: Both films end with critical mysteries unsolved. How will Marty escape 1955? Will Han survive? These major questions are left hanging, with the filmmakers expecting us to buy another ticket to learn the answers.
- **Open-Ended Plots**: The films halt abruptly in the middle of the protagonists' journeys. Viewers are left without any sense of resolution.
- **Minimal Emotional Closure**: Characters' emotional arcs are incomplete. Luke faces uncertainty about Vader, Han Solo is trapped in carbonite. And Marty still struggles to change history. Without any real resolution of characters' inner difficulties, audiences feel unsatisfied.
- **Lack of Foreshadowing**: The endings provide little indication of how the next films will resolve the cliffhangers. Viewers are left with more questions than clues about what comes next. This leaves audiences grasping at straws rather than waiting in eager anticipation.

A good cliffhanger requires a commitment from storytellers to provide satisfying payoffs for audiences. Without that, they only frustrate readers and viewers.

Fixing a bad cliffhanger involves understanding what elements are missing—from unanswered questions to incomplete character arcs—and providing those elements of resolution and closure before ending that installment of the story.

But take heart: committed storytellers can redeem even the most irritating of cliffhangers. Just be sure to do it before you turn in your final draft of your novel. Readers will thank you and they'll come back for more.

BEYOND THE SCREEN QUESTIONS

- Does your current cliffhanger ending leave any major questions unanswered for readers? Make a list and consider how you could provide more resolution.
- Are any of your protagonist's important story arcs or character arcs still incomplete at the current ending? How could you resolve those arcs more thoroughly?
- What foreshadowing or setup could you add earlier in the book to hint at how the next installment will resolve the current cliffhanger? Make a list of possibilities.
- Have you fully developed the themes and overall story arc you want your series to explore, or are you relying too much on the cliffhanger to motivate writing the next book?
- What specific revisions to your current ending could you make now to avoid frustrating readers and motivate them to pick up the next book in the series? Outline those changes.

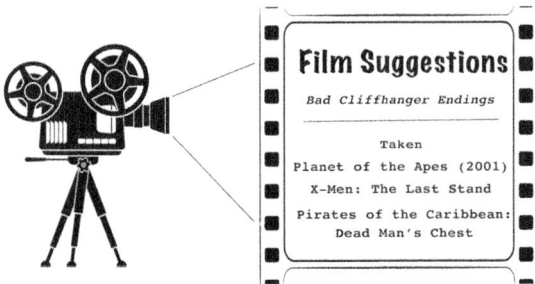

Film Suggestions

Bad Cliffhanger Endings

Taken
Planet of the Apes (2001)
X-Men: The Last Stand
Pirates of the Caribbean:
Dead Man's Chest

PRINCIPLE #12

TAKE A BREAK

WE'RE at about the halfway point in the book, so this might be a good time to take a break.

While the rest of this book extolls the virtues of working and being creative and getting things done, let's take a moment to take a moment.

It's a good habit to get into.

There's real value in stepping away from your work—for an hour, a day, a week, a month—to let your brain cells refresh.

As Jack Nicholson (and Stephen King and Stanley Kubrick) taught us in *The Shining*: "All work and no play makes Jack a dull boy."

Or, from a slightly sunnier perspective, consider Ferris Bueller's take on the topic (via screenwriter John Hughes in *Ferris Bueller's Day Off*): "Life moves pretty fast. You don't stop and look around once in a while, you could miss it."

Some filmic examples of the value of taking a break, no matter how short:

While he was directing *sex, lies and videotape*, Steven Soderbergh not only took off one day a week ... he also often spent that day getting lost in other people's movies. Here's how he recorded it in his production journal: "Day off felt good. Saw *Tucker: The Man and His Dream*, which (I'd) been dying to see."

Even today, many movies later, he still sees value in setting a project aside—at least for a while—to refresh and recharge.

"I'm more and more finding ways to create pockets of time to step away, so that I can come back and be less precious," Soderbergh told me. "I think the biggest lesson I learned over the years, especially with the first four films, is that preciousness—thinking too highly of your own material—is to be actively attacked."

One way that Soderbergh learned to step away—while remaining productive—is to have several movies in various stages of development at the same time.

"The benefit of having several projects going at once is that I move from projects on a day-by-day or night-by-night basis," he explained. "It keeps everything fresh. You never get bored with what you're doing and it doesn't feel like an obligation. You come back to something and say, 'Oh my God, why is <u>that</u> in the film?'"

Filmmaker Darren Aronofsky agrees that the long hours of writing, scouting, money-raising and pre-production ... followed by weeks of grueling 18-hour days of shooting ... followed by weeks or months of painstaking editing ... can take a physical, emotional and creative toll on a filmmaker.

During that process, you have to find ways to recharge your batteries. For Aronofsky—like Soderbergh—nothing does that better than taking a few hours off to see a movie.

His production diary for *pi* has one chapter entitled, *Some-*

times You Gotta Just Go See A Movie. In it, he notes: "I gave the editing crew the weekend off. After a fantastic push, the crew has earned it. We're all a bit exhausted, and a break is exactly what I needed. Today I will go see Woo's *Face-Off* and hopefully have a good time. I am broke."

So be willing to step away from time to time.

And if you don't believe me, here's what Maya Angelou observed: "Each person deserves a day in which no problems are confronted, no solutions searched for."

This idea is echoed by Alan Cohen, who wrote "There is virtue in work and there is virtue in rest. Use both and overlook neither."

While work and creativity are important, taking a break is just as crucial. Letting your brain cells refresh can work wonders. So, don't forget to step away from time to time, catch a movie, read a book, or just take the dog for a walk. As you do, you'll also be recharging your batteries.

Embrace this balance between work and rest, and you'll find yourself coming back stronger and less "precious" about your creations.

BEYOND THE SCREEN QUESTIONS

- Reflect on your writing process: Do you tend to work non-stop, or have you allowed yourself dedicated breaks to recharge?
- Consider the last time you took a break from your novel writing. What activities did you engage in during that time?

- Have you ever felt "precious" about your writing, and how has it affected your creativity?
- Think about ways you can create "pockets of time" for yourself to step away from your current project. What activities or hobbies could you incorporate into those breaks?
- Imagine having multiple writing projects in various stages of development. How could this approach help keep your creativity fresh and engaged?

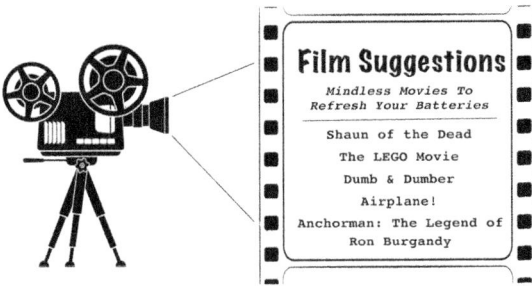

Film Suggestions

Mindless Movies To Refresh Your Batteries

Shaun of the Dead

The LEGO Movie

Dumb & Dumber

Airplane!

Anchorman: The Legend of Ron Burgandy

PRINCIPLE #13

CONCISE CONVOS: THE ART OF MOVIE DIALOGUE

A READER once commented to me that I must enjoy writing screenplays over writing novels, "because movies have tons more dialogue."

However, that's simply not true.

The word count of a screenplay can vary, but it's generally believed that a typical screenplay page contains approximately 150-200 words. Given the 'one page per minute' rule of thumb in screenwriting, a standard feature film script (which is usually between 90 and 120 pages) would therefore contain roughly between 14,000 and 24,000 words.

For comparison, most novels run from 50,000 to 70,000 words or more.

So, it follows that, generally speaking, movies have a lot less dialogue than most novels.

A limited streaming series — eight to ten hours — might have as much dialogue as a novel. But a standard two-hour movie simply doesn't have that much dialogue, compared to a book.

Screenwriting requires a tight, efficient use of dialogue due to time constraints, as well as the visual and auditory nature of the medium.

Which means whatever dialogue a movie does have needs to be tight. Every line, every word needs to be there for a reason.

In my mind, dialogue serves one of three purposes:

-It advances the plot/increases the tension

-It establishes, reveals and builds character.

-And from time to time it's funny and entertains.

If it can do all three at once, it's great dialogue.

And the real trick with great dialogue is that it needs to <u>sound</u> real, when it isn't real at all. Listen to actual conversations throughout your day and you'll hear just how little actual dialogue resembles fictional dialogue. In reality, people aren't that glib or able to organize their thoughts that well.

But great fictional dialogue is able to persuade us that what we're hearing is real, spilling forth readily from the minds and mouths of our characters.

One of my favorite examples of great film dialogue is from the movie *Tootsie*. I'm going to put the whole scene in here for you to read, because it really demonstrates how dialogue can advance the plot … establish, build, and reveal character … and also be terribly entertaining at the same time.

The *Tootsie* screenplay is by Murray Schisgal and Larry Gelbart, with the story by Don McGuire and Larry Gelbart. Elaine May also reportedly did uncredited script doctoring, so she may have contributed to this scene as well. (The mention of "Strindberg in the Park" has a very Elaine May feel to it.)

Here's a YouTube link to the scene (with no promises that it's still working when you read this). I've also included it in the Notes section: https://youtu.be/BnHqiipcw6g

INT. AGENT'S OFFICE - DAY

GEORGE

Michael, can you wait outside, please? I'm talking to the Coast.

MICHAEL

This is a coast, too, George. New York is a coast too!

GEORGE

Wait a minute.

(releases "hold;" then, into phone)

Margret, get him back, will you? I cut myself off. Now what is it, Michael?

MICHAEL

Terry Bishop is doing "Iceman Cometh." Didn't you promise to set me up for that part? Am I wrong? Didn't you tell me I was going to be able to read for that part? Aren't you my agent?

GEORGE

Stuart Pressman wants a name.

MICHAEL

Oh, I see. Terry Bishop is a name?

GEORGE

No. Michael Dorsey is a name. When you want to send a steak back, Michael Dorsey is a name. Wait, wait, wait. You always do that to me. That was a rotten thing to say and I know it. Let me start all over again. Terry Bishop is on a soap opera. Millions of people watch him every day. He's known.

MICHAEL

And that qualifies him to ruin "Iceman Cometh?" You know I can act circles around that guy. I already played that part in Minneapolis!

GEORGE

If Stuart Pressman wants a name, that's his affair. I know this will disgust you, Michael, but a lot of people are in this business to make money.

MICHAEL

Don't make me out like some flake, George, I am in this business to make money, too.

GEORGE

Oh, really? The Harlem Theatre for the Blind? Strindberg in the Park? The People's Workshop in Syracuse?

MICHAEL

Okay, now wait a minute: I did nine plays in eight months up in Syracuse! I happened to get great reviews from the New York critics! Not that that's why I did it—

GEORGE

— No, of course not. God forbid you should lose your standing as a cult failure.

MICHAEL

Do you think I'm a failure, George? Is that what you're saying?

GEORGE

I will not get sucked into this discussion. I will not.

MICHAEL

Okay, look, I sent you a play to read, that my roommate wrote. It had a great part in it for me. Did you read it?

GEORGE

Where the hell do you come off sending me your roommate's play for you to star in? I'm your agent, not your mother. I'm not supposed to find plays for you to star in it. I'm supposed to field offers. And that's what I do!

MICHAEL

Field offers? Who told you that? The agent-fairy? That was a significant piece of work, I could be terrific in it.

GEORGE

Nobody is going to do that play.

MICHAEL

Why?

GEORGE

Because it's a downer! No one is going to produce a play about a couple who move back to Love Canal!

MICHAEL

But that actually happened!

GEORGE

Who gives a shit! Nobody wants to pay $20 to watch people living next to chemical waste! They can see that in New Jersey.

MICHAEL

Ok, ok, I don't want to argue about this now, I'm going to raise the $8,000 myself so I can produce his play. I want you to send me up for anything. I don't care what it is! I will do dog commercials on television, I will do radio voice-overs.

GEORGE

Michael, I can't put you up for any of that.

MICHAEL

Why not?

GEORGE

Because no one will hire you.

MICHAEL

Oh, that's not true, man! I bust my ass to get a part right! And you know I do.

GEORGE

Yes, and you bust everyone else's ass too. That's what you do. A guy's got four weeks to put on a play — you think he wants to sit and argue about whether or not Tolstoy can walk when he's dying, or walk while he's talking, or sing while he's walking—

MICHAEL

That was two years ago, and that guy was an idiot.

GEORGE

They can't all be idiots, Michael. You argue with everyone. You've got one of the worst reputations in this town. Nobody will hire you.

MICHAEL

Are you saying that nobody in New York will work with me?

GEORGE

No, no. That's too limiting. Nobody in Hollywood wants to work with you either. I can't even send you up for a commercial. You played a tomato for 30 seconds and they went a half day over because you wouldn't sit down!

MICHAEL

Yes. It wasn't logical.

GEORGE

You were a tomato! A tomato doesn't have logic! A tomato can't move!

MICHAEL

That's what I said! So, if it can't move, how's he going to sit down, George?! I was a stand-up tomato. A juicy, sexy beefsteak tomato. Nobody does vegetables like me! I did an evening of vegetables off-Broadway. I did the best tomato, the best cucumber! I did an endive salad that knocked the critics on their ass!

GEORGE

Michael … I'm trying to stay calm here. You … are a wonderful actor.

MICHAEL

Thank you.

GEORGE

But you're too much trouble. Get some therapy.

MICHAEL

(quietly determined)

Okay, thanks. I'm going to raise $8,000 and I'm going to do Jeff's play.

GEORGE

(shaking his head)

Michael, you aren't going to raise .25 cents

(slowly)

No one will hire you.

MICHAEL

Oh yeah?

· · ·

That is just a terrific scene.

-It tells us all we need to know about Michael Dorsey

-It clearly establishes his relationship with his agent (helping to set up the first Dorothy Michaels/Agent scene later).

-It advances the plot by telling us why Michael can't get work and why he must get work to produce his friend's play.

I mentioned *Tootsie* in the first book, *The Popcorn Principles*, for the way in which it cuts out the shoe leather at the end of this scene, cutting directly from Michael saying "Oh, yeah?" to him fully coifed and dressed as Dorothy Michaels.

This scene—in fact, the whole movie—is a master class in writing dialogue, shaping character via dialogue, establishing different voices via the dialogue … it's just a great, great movie.

However, dialogue is not always the answer.

Sometimes it's the things the characters DON'T say that are important.

Knowing when to let your characters talk, and when to let them be silent is an important skill to develop.

A great example of using silence to convey character and plot comes at the end of *Big Night*, a movie starring Stanley Tucci and Tony Shalhoub. The screenplay was by Stanley Tucci & Joseph Tropiano.

It's the final scene in the movie. It's the morning after the Big Night. Two brothers have had a terrific argument, where years of anger and disappointment have boiled to the surface.

Here's a YouTube link to the scene (with no promises that it's still working when you read this). I've also included the link in the Notes section: https://youtu.be/oerP7FRMWa8

EXT. OCEAN - DAWN

The sun is coming up, reflecting on the grey waves.

CUT TO

INT. PARADISE KITCHEN - DAWN

SECONDO enters from the dining room. He spots CHRIS-
TIANO, who is asleep on the butcher block. SECONDO moves
to the stove. He takes down a frying pan, puts in some olive oil,
and turns on the stove.

CHRISTIANO wakes up.

SECONDO
     Are you hungry?

CHRISTIANO nods his head "yes." He starts to get down from
the butcher block, but SECONDO gestures for him to stop.

SECONDO
     I'll do it.

CHRISTIANO sits on the butcher block with his legs dangling.
He watches as SECONDO deftly chops some garlic and parsley.
His chopping is effortless, beautiful. He adds these to the oil. He
takes two eggs and breaks them into a bowl simultaneously with
both hands, then two more, puts in a drop of milk, and whips
them with a whisk and adds them to the pan.

SECONDO takes some eggs, puts them on a plate, and gives the
plate to CHRISTIANO. Then he makes one for himself. They
begin to eat.

They HEAR the back door open. SECONDO turns. PRIMO comes in. SECONDO and PRIMO nod at each other.

SECONDO puts down his plate, makes a plate for PRIMO, and brings it to him. PRIMO nods.

SECONDO goes back to his plate and begins eating again.

HOLD ON the three of them, eating their eggs like hungry children.

BLACKOUT.

That scene, with hardly a word of dialogue in it, tells you all you need to know about their relationship—who they are to each other and how they will be together until the end, despite their differences.

Movies teach us a lot about concise yet meaningful dialogue —making words matter and giving each character their own unique voice. Practice being stingy with words but generous with subtext for your characters.

The more you refine your dialogue skills, the more genuine and powerful their words will become—imbuing them with a life of their own that lingers long after readers finish your novel.

BEYOND THE FILM QUESTIONS

- Identify one example of dialogue in your current work-in-progress that could be tightened or removed. How might shortening or cutting that dialogue altogether improve the scene?
- Does your dialogue primarily serve to advance the plot and build character? Or does some of it feel

indulgent? Circle or highlight one line of dialogue that you could cut without losing any meaning.

- Select a passage of dialogue in your novel with at least three characters speaking. For each line, identify whether it reveals character, drives the plot forward, or entertains the reader. What could you cut or change to optimize those functions?

- Are there any moments in your novel where silence would be more powerful than words? Select one such place and write a new paragraph describing what is communicated through characters' nonverbal reactions.

- Do you find yourself struggling to make your characters' dialogue sound "real"? What one step could you take to improve, such as listening to actual conversations or analyzing well-written dialogue in books and movies?

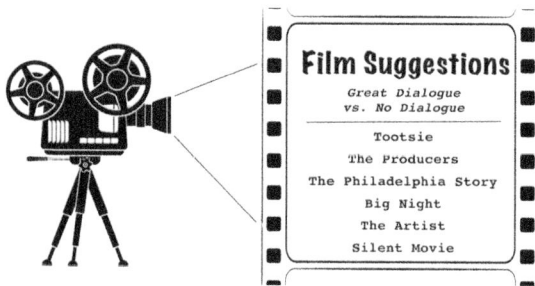

Film Suggestions

Great Dialogue vs. No Dialogue

Tootsie

The Producers

The Philadelphia Story

Big Night

The Artist

Silent Movie

PRINCIPLE #14
MIXING FACT AND FICTION

BLENDING fact and fiction in historical storytelling requires a delicate balance. Responsible fictionalization of history demands meticulous research, focus on emotional rather than literal truths, transparency about changes made, and potentially fictionalizing characters to avoid inaccuracies that offend.

Nicholas Meyer is a novelist, screenwriter, and filmmaker known for his Sherlock Holmes novel, *The Seven-Per-Cent Solution*, his work on a couple of the best *Star Trek* movies, his devastating TV movie, *The Day After*, and his television adaptation of the life of Houdini.

For Meyer, dramatizing history requires balancing authenticity with the storytelling necessity of embellishment. As he explained to me, "There's no such thing as fiction; all fiction ultimately can be traced back to something real.

"I'll give you two examples off the top of my head. One: *Moby Dick* was based on a real whale called Mocha Dick because of his color. And, as Heinrich Schliemann proved when he discovered Troy, most legends, most myths have their origins somewhere in the mists of time, in some kind of reality. It turns out there <u>was</u> a place called Troy."

However, deciding how much creative license to take and

"when you cross a line and start inventing things out of whole cloth" is a challenge Meyer has grappled with in his own work.

"The problem is that people are neither taught, nor do they read history anymore. We are not taught civics. We are not taught history. Nobody knows anything and so, by default, movies and television are where we get our history. And that history is not always truthful. It is dramatized.

"For example, in the Academy Award-winning movie, *The Deer Hunter*, we learned that the North Vietnamese made American prisoners of war in Vietnam play Russian roulette. There is no evidence, no historical evidence that they ever did any such thing. And yet, if you're getting your history from the movies, that's what you see.

"You have to always be looking over your own shoulder when you are dramatizing history and realizing that, yes, you can tell a story with scope, dates and characters. But what's the point where you cross a line and start inventing things out of whole cloth?"

Meyer offered another example: "Was Richard the Third really the monster that Shakespeare portrays? Now, remember, Shakespeare is writing for the granddaughter of the man who killed Richard the Third and usurped his throne and called himself king. You could make a very different case that [Henry the Seventh] was a scumbag and that Richard was not. But Shakespeare was in business. The Globe Theatre was a money-making operation. And Henry the Seventh's granddaughter was the Queen of England. So, there are a lot of variables here."

When scripting his Houdini biopic, Meyer had to make judgments about what was factual vs. fictional. "It's a question of how much we owe to fact and how much we get to mush around and dramatize?" he noted. But creating fiction based on real events has risks.

Dan Futterman, the Academy Award-nominated screenwriter of *Capote*, discovered this when adapting the famous author's life for film. Several moments in the film present scenes between Capote and his editor, William Shawn, discussing what would become Capote's masterwork, *In Cold Blood*. Once the film was released, Futterman was approached by members of Shawn's family.

"I recently have had correspondence with Wallace Shawn, who is William Shawn's son," Futterman told me. "He and his brother are not terribly happy about the way William Shawn is portrayed in the film.

"I knew that Capote had three different editors involved in the book. One was William Shawn of *The New Yorker*, one was Bennett Cerf at Random House, and then when Cerf retired, a guy named Joe Fox took over. That just seemed too confusing to present in a movie. We needed one editor, and I chose that to be William Shawn, and he would do everything that all the other guys did as well. That upset Wallace and I feel badly about it. If I were able to go back, I would try to solve it."

For Futterman, it wasn't just about the dramatic necessity; there was more to the choice he had made in his writing.

"What you encounter is that, even if the people have died, there is a moral debt owed to them in terms of trying to adhere as strictly as possible to the truth. It's something I tried to be very conscious of, but in this particular case, I think I came up short."

One option in a situation like this is to simply fictionalize the character with a made-up name; all the same actions and dialogue would take place, but it wouldn't be assigned to an actual person. But that wasn't something Futterman considered while writing the script—although he would make that choice if the situation arose again in the future.

"It didn't occur to me at the time that any of the things I had him doing could possibly be upsetting to anybody. But that was my own take and I see now why his sons are upset," Futterman recalled. "Looking back now, I would try to find a way to fix it."

As writers, we have the opportunity to reimagine history, to illuminate lasting human truths. But we must do so responsibly. This means:

- Do meticulous research to separate probable facts from embellishments.
- Focus on emotional truths over literal accuracy but ground your story in authentic history.
- Be transparent about where you've shaped events for dramatic purposes.

"If you read the history or a biography, you understand that in good faith, efforts have been made to lay out the facts," Meyer explained. "But when you read a historical novel, you understand that the facts have been mushed around and dramatized, that the author has assumed the dramatist's privilege, his prerogative, to help things along.

"There's an Italian phrase, *Se non è vero, è ben trovato.* 'If it didn't happen that way, it should have.'

"I'll give you another example: Queen Elizabeth the First and her cousin and rival, Mary Queen of Scots—whom Elizabeth subsequently had beheaded—never met in real life. They'd never met. But of all the 4,622 movies, plays, operas, novellas, ballets, whatever, they always meet.

"Because it ain't cool if they don't meet. It makes a better story."

BEYOND THE SCREEN QUESTIONS

- How have you researched factual events for your novel? What additional research could you do to ensure accuracy? Make a plan for that research.
- Identify three facts or details in your novel that are embellished or fictionalized. How could you root those elements more firmly in actual history?
- Does your novel accurately convey the emotional truths of the time period and events it depicts? What details could you add to strengthen that emotional resonance?
- Consider major characters in your novel based on real people. If applicable, how could you fictionalize those characters to avoid inaccuracies that might upset loved ones?
- What frustrates you most about the challenge of blending fact and fiction in your novel? How can you work through that struggle productively?

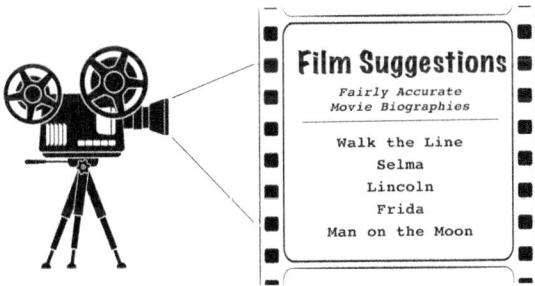

Film Suggestions

Fairly Accurate Movie Biographies

Walk the Line
Selma
Lincoln
Frida
Man on the Moon

PRINCIPLE #15
PLAY WITH STRUCTURE

THE BEAUTY of fiction writing is the freedom to experiment that it offers. Why stick to traditional structures when you can shake things up and surprise readers in delightful ways? Many classic books have become classics partially because they upended traditional structures:

- *Ulysses* by James Joyce is written in a stream of consciousness style, moving fluidly between the thoughts of multiple characters throughout a single day in Dublin. The novel plays with timelines, flashbacks and narrative perspective in innovative ways which in many ways mirror the flow of the human mind.
- *House of Leaves* by Mark Z. Danielewski is structured as a commentary on a fictional documentary film. The text features footnotes within footnotes, multiple typefaces and unusual layouts that defy the standard book form. The experimental use of structure enhances the theme of discovering hidden mysteries within the ordinary world.

- *Life After Life* by Kate Atkinson employs the "what if?" premise to its fullest, following a character who repeatedly relives the timeline of her life from different points, altering the narrative each time. The story zigzags across decades, timelines and possible worlds in a dazzling demonstration of the power of reshaping form to reflect thematic content.
- *Catch-22* by Joseph Heller employs an absurd, circular structure that mirrors the illogicality and bureaucracy of the novel's central theme of the madness of war. The chronology zigzags back and forth between past and present in crazy, mirthful ways.

Books haven't cornered the market on playing with structure. Movies have long pushed the limits of narrative form, jumping across timelines, reversing stories, and remixing genres. Filmmakers aren't afraid to think differently about structure—and neither should you.

Take inspiration from these movies that playfully subvert conventions:

- *Pulp Fiction* serves up its story in a mixed-up chronological order, allowing the reveals of the plot to truly pack a punch. A perfect example of how rearranging the parts can transform the whole.
- *Memento* tells its story backwards from the very first scene, challenging viewers to piece together the mystery by working backwards from the climax.
- *Citizen Kane* begins in inventive fashion with a satirical fake newsreel that sets the stage for the film's investigative flashbacks and nonlinear structure. As characters reminisce about Kane, we are transported

back in time through flashbacks to pivotal moments that shaped his life. By employing the framing newsreel and flashbacks, *Citizen Kane* exhibits narrative sophistication well ahead of its time.

- *Sliding Doors* shows how one single decision can create two starkly different realities for its characters. A thought experiment made cinematic through innovative story structure.

\|\|\|/ \|\|\|/ \|\|\|/

If you've learned one thing from these examples, let it be this: bend the forms and throw structure out the window if it pleases you! Experiment, play, have fun—for that is where truly original storytelling is born.

The movies (and books) discussed here show that unconventional structure—used well—can yield a story that both surprises and delights readers in equal measure. From *Ulysses* zigzagging across streams of consciousness to *Pulp Fiction* serving up nonlinearity with a twist, these examples prove that rules were made for breaking—if doing so serves the higher purposes of theme, enjoyment and truth. *(We'll examine this concept of the value of rule breaking in more detail in Principle #19 – Rules Are Made to Be Broken.)*

Experiment, play, and have faith that surprises will emerge. For as James Joyce said, "The modern writer must be an adventurer above all, willing to take every risk, and be prepared to founder in his effort if need be. In other words, we must write dangerously."

BEYOND THE SCREEN QUESTIONS

- In what ways is your current story structure either traditional or unconventional? What are the strengths and limitations of this structure?
- What alternate structures could you experiment with to stir things up—nonlinear timelines, multiple storylines, flashbacks, framing devices, etc.?
- How could changing the structure enhance or amplify specific themes in your story?
- What rules or conventions of structure currently feel constraining to you? Which could you playfully break to see what new possibilities emerge?
- If you threw structure out the window altogether, what shape might your story ultimately take? What intuitions does your creativity have that you're not listening to?

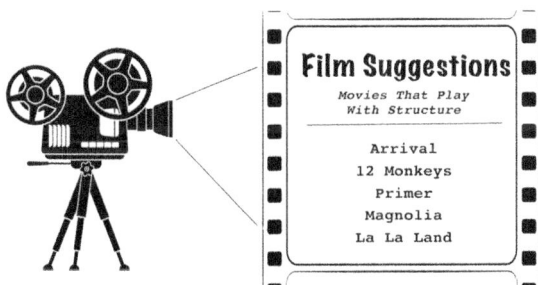

Film Suggestions

*Movies That Play
With Structure*

Arrival
12 Monkeys
Primer
Magnolia
La La Land

PRINCIPLE #16

MAKING THEM CRY

ONE QUESTION I'm occasionally asked by readers of *The Popcorn Principles* is: How can I make readers cry when they read my books the way they do when watching certain movies?

This is a challenge, because films have some distinct advantages over novels when it comes to eliciting strong emotions. Movies can rely on swelling music, close-up reaction shots, talented actors conveying heartbreak with a subtle facial expression, and other techniques not available to novelists.

So how can writers compete with all that?

In my experience, the most effective way for a novel to make readers cry is to create compelling, relatable characters that readers care deeply about. When those characters face tragedy or are in jeopardy, readers will empathize and may shed tears.

Think of classics like *Charlotte's Web* or *Old Yeller* that had many readers crying into their books. It wasn't elaborate prose or plot twists that got the tears flowing—it was readers' emotional connection to the characters. When Charlotte died or Old Yeller was shot, we cried because they had become like old friends.

The key is to make sure your characters are multi-dimensional and emotionally resonant before you put them through the wringer. Give them hopes, fears, and relationships that readers recognize and relate to. The more readers care, the more impact any tragedy will have.

Putting characters in serious physical jeopardy certainly helps raise the emotional stakes. But you can go even further by having the jeopardy threaten their close relationships as well.

In the movie *World War Z*, early audience reactions were lukewarm. So, the filmmakers changed the focus from a global apocalypse to one man's quest to save his family. They literally threw out the final third of the film and started over on the climax, following Brad Pitt as he raced to save his family from the zombie hordes. They made the scale considerably smaller, but in so doing, they made the emotions deeper.

You can use a similar technique by having the core tragedy in your novel—whether death or something else—also threaten to sever a close character relationship that readers have come to care about. Raise the emotional stakes along with the plot stakes and you'll get the emotional reaction you desire.

In an early version of *Fatal Attraction*, test audiences sympathized too much with Glenn Close's character, so her death (a suicide) was reshot. The new ending had Close literally attacking Michael Douglas's family, with his wife pulling the trigger on the gun which kills Close. Because they had shifted the peril to a more personal level, audiences became more involved in the outcome.

Similarly, the original script for *Rocky* had the boxer accepting money to throw the fight against Apollo Creed. Audiences hated this cynical ending, so it was changed to have Rocky go the distance in an honest fight.

Another technique: Films often strategically place emotional cues earlier in the story to set up stronger reactions later. Pop songs with personal meaning or symbolic objects associated with relationships are examples. When the cue appears again at a tragic moment, the emotion comes flooding back.

Near the beginning of *Titanic*, Jack draws a portrait of Rose wearing the Heart of the Ocean necklace. When old Rose takes the necklace from her pocket at the end to drop it in the ocean, it's a poignant callback to their doomed relationship.

In *Terminator 2*, John teaches the T-800 to give a thumbs up. When the T-800 gives one last thumbs up at the end, it's a poignant callback to their relationship.

Novels can do something similar by planting memories, keepsakes, or other emotional reminders early on that you can invoke again later for maximum impact. If you establish an object as having deep meaning for a character, its presence during a tragedy will hit readers that much harder.

The element of surprise can also make an emotional scene hit harder. (Warning: major spoilers ahead!)

In *Psycho*, Hitchcock makes us care about Norman Bates, so that we sympathize with him even after he works to cover up his mother's murder of Marion Crane. Consequently, the surprise twist at the end of the film has double emotional impact.

Other films have achieved that effect as well. In *The Usual Suspects*, we sympathize with Verbal Kint throughout—he is abused by virtually every character in the film at some point—until the twist ending reveals he is really the villain, Keyser Soze.

In *Memento*, our sympathies change as we learn more about Leonard's questionable past through the reverse storyline.

And in *The Sixth Sense*, the audience sympathizes with Malcolm's relationship with Cole, until the late revelation that Malcolm is actually a ghost. I don't think the film would have had the impact it did if Malcolm's relationship with Cole hadn't been as artfully crafted.

Can a novelist make their readers cry? Yes, I think they can elicit tears by making readers care deeply about characters, threatening relationships along with lives, planting emotional cues early on, and surprising readers with poignant plot twists. Execute these things skillfully, and readers will need tissues handy when they reach the end of your story.

BEYOND THE SCREEN QUESTIONS

- Which of your characters do readers care about most right now? What could you do to deepen that emotional connection?
- Is there a traumatic event coming up for a character? How can you raise the emotional stakes by threatening their relationships as well?
- What symbolic objects or memories could you establish earlier that might take on more meaning during an emotional scene later?
- Are there any opportunities to surprise readers with poignant plot twists regarding your characters?
- Are you being honest and specific when writing emotional scenes, instead of vague or overly melodramatic?

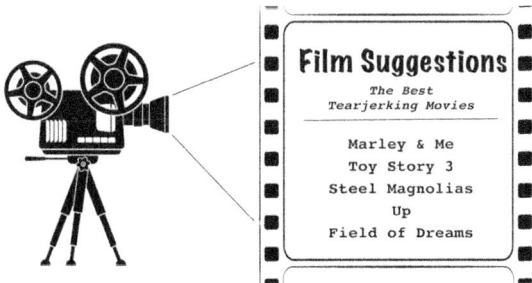

Film Suggestions

The Best Tearjerking Movies

Marley & Me
Toy Story 3
Steel Magnolias
Up
Field of Dreams

PRINCIPLE #17
BE OPEN TO THE MOMENT

I WAS lucky enough to interview the director Lesli Linka Glatter. She is known for her work on dramatic series like *Homeland, Mad Men*, and *Twin Peaks*. After starting her career choreographing dance sequences for film and TV, Glatter transitioned to directing in the 1980s, getting her first big break on Steven Spielberg's TV series, *Amazing Stories*.

"That was like my film school," Glatter told me. "It was an extraordinary opportunity, and he was beyond generous."

But it was while working on the classic TV series *Twin Peaks* that Glatter had a revelatory moment which has stuck with her to this day.

"I directed four episodes and that was another huge turning point for me," Glatter recounted. But the true revelation was something she had seen in the show's pilot episode.

"There was a scene in the pilot for the show in which Michael Ontkean is talking to Kyle MacLachlan. It's in a bank, in a room where you look at your safety deposit box. In the middle of the scene, on this table, was this moose head. They play the whole scene in this room, and no one ever refers to the moose head. The scene is incredible."

That scene—and that moose—stayed with Glatter. And when

she finally had the chance to meet with the show's co-creator, David Lynch, she couldn't help but ask about how that image had come about.

"So, when I got to know David, I went up to him and said, 'How did you ever get the idea to put the moose head on the table?' He looked at me like I was kind of crazy, and he said, 'It was there.'

"And I said, 'What do you mean it was there?' He said, 'The set decorator was going to hang it on the wall,' and David said to the decorator, 'Leave the moose head.'

"Something just cracked open in my brain," Glatter explained. "Be sure you're open to the moment. Be sure you see the moose head on the table. Don't try to control things so much that you're not open to what's happening in the moment.

"That was a great lesson and a huge turning point for me," Glatter said.

Like Glatter, novelists can benefit tremendously by being open to creative accidents and the moments of inspiration that come from real life.

Here are some ways writers can harness that mindset:

- When going about your daily routine, purposefully look for oddities, encounters, or overheard conversations that spark novel story or character ideas. Carry a small notebook to jot down inspiration.
- Don't over-plan every story beat and plot point. Allow yourself room to spontaneously incorporate interesting details or go down surprising tangents.
- Try writing sessions based entirely on stream-of-consciousness writing or automatic writing to tap into your subconscious thoughts and perspectives.

- Use character naming tricks like basing names on interesting gravesites or shop signs you pass in your travels. Let these accidental details influence your writing.
- Go to public places to write occasionally for the ambient noise and activity. Allow these to seep into your writing when helpful.
- In dialogue, sometimes let characters go "off script" into humorous or emotional tangents that feel genuine versus planned.
- Don't edit or censor yourself in early drafts—unusual imagery, descriptions, or plot developments that just pop into your head often lead to something special.

For Glatter, there have been two pivotal lessons she's learned in her career.

"From Steven Spielberg I learned, 'Do your homework and never pretend you know what you don't, because someone is going to be there who knows and you're going to get caught,'" Glatter recalled. "Which was all about planning and control.

"And from David I learned, 'Yes, do all of that, but be sure you're open to the moment.'"

BEYOND THE SCREEN QUESTIONS

- Do you carry a small notebook or voice recorder to capture spur-of-the-moment story ideas and details from daily life?
- Could you incorporate more real-world randomness into your story by basing character names on gravestones or signs you see?
- When was the last time you wrote stream-of-consciously just to tap into unexpected thoughts and perspectives?

- Can you identify any recent dialogue scenes where characters went "off script" into more genuine tangents?
- Do you tend to heavily edit and censor your early drafts? Or do you allow unusual ideas and descriptions to flow freely?

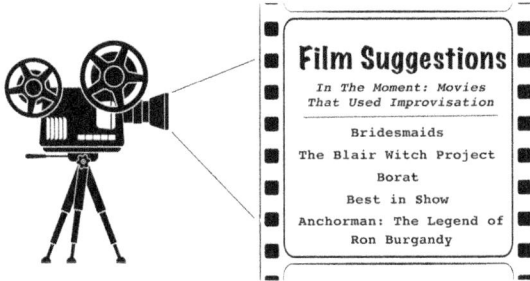

Film Suggestions

In The Moment: Movies That Used Improvisation

Bridesmaids

The Blair Witch Project

Borat

Best in Show

Anchorman: The Legend of Ron Burgandy

PRINCIPLE #18
CREATE EVERY DAY

DON'T PANIC. The title of this chapter is <u>Create</u> Every Day. Not <u>Write</u> Every Day.

So, relax.

I know there are those of you who do, in fact, write every day. Good for you. Godspeed.

But for many of us, that sort of pressure makes writing harder rather than easier.

Instead, what we're looking at in this principle is the benefit of <u>creating</u> every day. Finding a way, on a daily basis, to stretch our creative muscles and keep our imaginations limber.

Doing this will ensure that—when we do sit down to write—we're primed to do our best work.

I first heard about this concept from filmmaker and editor Roger Nygard (*Suckers, The Office, Curb Your Enthusiasm, Veep*).

So let me turn this chapter over to Roger. This is what he had to say on the topic:

I remember reading a study once—I think way back in college—how there was this nursing home where they had 100 residents, and they gave everybody a plant.

To 50% of the residents, they said, "Here's a plant, we'll take care of it, you have no responsibility."

To the other 50%, they said, "Here's the plant, you need to water this and take care of it. It's your responsibility."

And the people with the responsibility for the plant lived longer.

Because they suddenly had a reason for being in their life.

It's about creation: they're creating life out of this plant and keeping it alive. And it's innate in us to create.

When human beings are not expressing creativity, they become depressed.

If you give someone who's depressed a piece of paper and say, "Take 10 minutes and draw a picture of a plant or a giraffe, just draw a picture," while they're drawing, the depression is not a part of their mental framework. Because they're expressing creativity, they have a purpose. Even if it's for those ten minutes.

So, you and I, we put forth that energy into a film or a product, ultimately, that has a larger result of some kind. We finish it, we show it to our community or social network, we get feedback. And then that self-perpetuating loop continues.

Some of that feedback is negative, some of its positive. But it's good to get any feedback. Because we're social creatures, we need that feedback.

We need to engage and be creative.

And that's a lesson that I learned from the beginning, from age seven until now: I enjoy the result of my labor, my creative labor daily. A little bit of that Minnesota work ethic is that if I don't put forth some effort during the day, I feel like a complete loser at the end of the day.

So, I have to have something to show for myself for the day, some work I put in, some results. Whether it's cleaning the garage, or writing a book, either one—or both—are immensely satisfying to have completed. To feel like I completed something today.

I can look back on myself and go, "Wow, I did that. I feel really good about myself."

It's a self-perpetuating process.

So how can we gain the satisfaction and fulfillment of creating, even when we don't write every day? As Roger mentioned, simple acts of creation can have surprising benefits.

Whether it's photographing something beautiful, drawing a portrait, composing a poem, playing an instrument, or dreaming up a story for your kids—engaging your creativity in any form is good for your soul. It reminds you of your capacity to imagine and build within your mind, your heart, and your hands.

The key is consistency: making some kind of creative output part of your daily ritual. Even if it's just for 10 or 15 minutes each morning with your coffee. That dedication and discipline will slowly build momentum. Ideas begat more ideas. Skills improve with practice. Confidence grows as you reinforce your identity as a creator.

Each time you create, something inside of you awakens. Your curiosity, your imagination, your joy. And those parts of yourself are exactly what your stories need most—whether you write them down today, tomorrow or next year.

BEYOND THE SCREEN QUESTIONS

- What are three simple forms of creative expression you enjoy and could incorporate on a daily basis? Make a list and choose one to commit to for this week.
- When in your day would be the most suitable time for a short creative ritual? Morning, lunch break, evening? Mark it on your calendar.

- How will you give yourself grace if you miss a day or aren't satisfied with the results? Remember, the act of creation itself is what matters most.
- Who is one person you could share your daily creative efforts with to keep yourself accountable? Reach out and ask them for support.
- What mindset shift helps you move from "I'm not good enough to create" to "I create, therefore I am"? Repeat this new mantra to yourself.

Film Suggestions

Movies & TV Shows
That Inspire Creativity

Toy Story

Ratatouille

Moonrise Kingdom

The Muppet Show

The Great British Bake-Off

PRINCIPLE #19

RULES ARE MADE TO BE BROKEN

"Learn the rules like a pro, so you can break them like an artist."
   —*Pablo Picasso*

LET'S chat for a moment or so about Roger Corman.

Roger Corman is legendary.

He's legendary for nurturing young talent. He gave early opportunities to filmmakers like Francis Ford Coppola, James Cameron, Martin Scorsese, and Ron Howard.

He's legendary for making low-budget genre films. He specialized in making thrillers, horror films and sci-fi movies on tiny budgets that still entertained audiences.

And he's legendary for being a strict taskmaster with his directors: no one dared to go over-time or over-budget on his films.

But he was also a realist and recognized that sometimes you had to bend the rules to get the job done.

This was one of the key concepts he offered up to potential directors during The Lunch, the legendary pre-shoot meal he had with anyone he was letting direct one of his movies. Director Jonathan Demme, who was about to direct *Caged Heat* for Corman, described it this way:

"The Lunch is where in the course of about an hour and a half (because time is money, too), you get what is, as far as I'm concerned, the equivalent of four years in film school, just machine gun. The rules and regulations of how to make a very interesting film from a directorial point of view. So, it was a spectacular moment in my life as a filmmaker to be able to spend that time. He even picked up the check!"

Although he laid out the rules of filmmaking at The Lunch, Corman also understood when those rules needed to be broken … or, at the very least, bent.

For example, on first-time director Peter Bogdanovich's film, *Targets*, the new director broke one of Corman's rules and shot several scenes in long, continuous takes without any coverage. (Coverage means shots you can cut away to, in order to tighten a scene in editing: a close up, a reaction shot, a POV shot and so on.)

"It went a little bit against my rules," Corman told me. "But on the other hand, all rules are made to be broken. I do like to get coverage, to get as much coverage as possible. Yet, at the same time, when you're on a very tight schedule, sometimes you have to sacrifice coverage. And when you do that, sometimes you can make a virtue out of necessity."

Corman understood an essential truth about creativity: sometimes the rules need to be broken in order to create something truly meaningful and original. This is just as true for novelists as it is for filmmakers.

As a writer, you've been taught all the accepted conventions of storytelling—following an archetypal narrative structure, incorporating proper scene and sequence construction, developing believable and multifaceted characters, and so on.

These rules serve an important purpose: they equip you with a fundamental toolset to craft a solid story.

But to create great art, you'll inevitably have to break some of the rules that initially shaped you. This can mean writing outside of a traditional hero's journey structure, using stream of consciousness or nonlinear storytelling, subverting character tropes, or even disregarding established rules of grammar and syntax.

The key is to first internalize the conventions—learn them like a pro, as Picasso suggested—so that you understand why they exist and what purpose they serve. This provides a foundation from which you can experiment and take creative risks. Only once you grasp the fundamentals can you begin to bend or break the rules like an artist.

So, as you write your novel, it's okay to follow the accepted rules of storytelling at first. Use them as a scaffolding to build your early drafts. But then, as your vision and voice emerge, allow yourself the freedom to experiment. Disregard rules that feel stale or restrictive to your authentic story.

Create the book that only you could write.

BEYOND THE SCREEN QUESTIONS

- What rules of craft feel most restrictive or stale for your unique story? Make a note to experiment by breaking those rules in your next draft.
- How closely have you followed a traditional 3-act or 5-act story structure so far? Consider ways you could modify or expand that structure to better suit your actual narrative.
- What risks could you take with structure, timeline, characterization or genre conventions in your next draft? Commit to trying at least one.

- How will you give yourself grace if some of your "rule breaking" doesn't work initially? Remember that experimenting is part of the creative process.
- What quote or mantra could help remind you that rules are tools meant to be transcended by artists? Write it down or post it as inspiration.

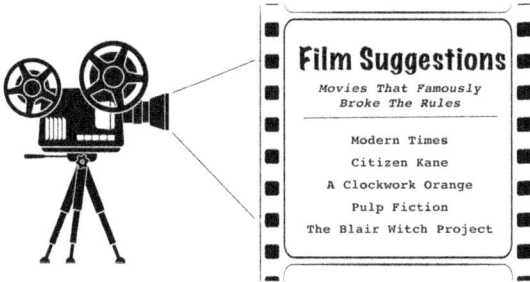

Film Suggestions

Movies That Famously Broke The Rules

Modern Times

Citizen Kane

A Clockwork Orange

Pulp Fiction

The Blair Witch Project

PRINCIPLE #20

SOON TO BE A MAJOR MOTION
PICTURE? NOT LIKELY, BUT ...

MANY AUTHORS DREAM of Hollywood adaptations of their work. Yet, in reality, very few books ever make that leap from page to screen.

Sadly, it's a real long shot.

With so many books published, any one novel struggles to stand out. Even with streaming services looking for more and more material, adapting books remains inefficient for producers. Unless that book (or author) already has a strong following, such as a multi-million-selling book or a million or more social media followers.

Self-published authors face steeper odds than traditionally published authors for one simple reason: big publishers have Rights departments who spend all their time trying to connect books with producers; indies don't have that advantage.

Steve Martin had a joke which reflects this quandary: "I can teach you how to not pay taxes on a million dollars. First, get a million dollars…"

That same lesson applies here—write a breakout hit that producers fight over, and your book will be turned into a movie. But that's rare and not something you can simply manifest.

Still, creative strategies exist, and analogs can be found in the movie world.

The making of the low-budget feature *Roger Dodger* is one such example.

In *Roger Dodger,* Campbell Scott plays a smooth-talking NYC ad man who tries to teach his awkward nephew (Jesse Eisenberg) how to pick up women on a wild night out that doesn't go as planned.

Writer/director Dylan Kidd explained the frustration he had getting *Roger Dodger* off the ground.

"My producer partner and I got to a stage where we realized, 'we're not going to get this movie made in the standard fashion,'" Kidd told me. "It's like that New York thing, where nobody ever finds an apartment by actually going through the real estate listings. It's always somebody you know; there's always some backdoor.

"So, really in a fit of insanity, thinking if I don't make this movie, I'm going to go crazy, I started carrying the script with me every day. I thought, 'Well, I live in New York, maybe I'll run into somebody.' And that's how it happened—two weeks after starting that routine of not leaving the house without the script, I walked into a café and there was (actor) Campbell Scott."

With Scott's interest and help, Kidd was able to get the film financed and produced.

Kidd acknowledges handing out unsolicited scripts risks litigation, but he was "so clueless." His advice: "Be really polite and make sure you really do have a killer part to offer." He went on to say, "This was a great role. If you feel like you have this great gift...it allows you to feel like you're not just disturbing this guy's lunch."

Kidd's story demonstrates how passion, luck and persistence

can pay off. So, while few authors will see big or small screen adaptations of their work, creative strategies do exist.

- Focus first on writing the best book possible. Pour your passion into the story, not into Hollywood hopes.
- Then, reach out humbly yet proactively. Dylan Kidd advised offering a "meaty" role only the right actor could do justice. He got lucky with Campbell Scott, but had a role that sparked Campbell's interest.
- Expect long odds. But don't rule out serendipity. You never know whose hands your novel may fall into, whose heart it may touch.

So, make it the best book possible. Then venture forth with patience, pragmatism and a bit of hope.

That's how Dylan Kidd made *Roger Dodger*: with a great role scripted for a great actor, persistence carrying the script everywhere, and luck literally running into the actor he sought.

Creative fire occasionally meets serendipity. Why not for your story too?

BEYOND THE SCREEN QUESTIONS

- Considering the odds against getting your book adapted into a movie or TV show, how might you manage your expectations while still maintaining hope for such an outcome?
- How can you ensure that your book stands out among the vast number of publications, increasing its chances of catching a producer's attention?
- What strategies can you adopt from the story of Dylan Kidd and *Roger Dodger* in your pursuit of getting your book adapted into a film or TV series?

- How can you create characters or roles in your book that would be appealing to actors, thereby increasing the likelihood of a successful adaptation?
- Reflecting on the principle of "creative fire occasionally meets serendipity," how might you prepare yourself to seize unexpected opportunities that could lead to your book's adaptation?

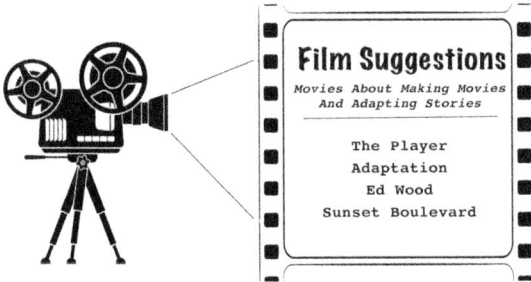

Film Suggestions

Movies About Making Movies And Adapting Stories

The Player
Adaptation
Ed Wood
Sunset Boulevard

PRINCIPLE #21
ANTICIPATE SUCCESS

AS A WRITER, you always want to keep your focus on your current project. But it doesn't hurt to have something in your hip pocket, particularly if your current project suddenly hits it big.

This idea is built into the DNA of Hollywood. Filmmakers have understood for years that it's a good idea to have another idea percolating before you release your latest project into the world.

That was the case with the low-budget classic, *Clerks*. Writer/director Kevin Smith and producer Scott Mosier were ready when opportunity suddenly knocked.

"We met (Hollywood producer) Jim Jacks at the closing ceremonies of Sundance," Mosier recalled, "and he asked us what we wanted to do next."

"And I said, *Mallrats*," Smith remembered. "Just out of nowhere. And they went with it; 'Oh yeah, that's funny!' Amazing."

"So, before *Clerks* ever came out, based on our meeting with Jim Jacks, we generated our second project," continued Mosier. "By the time *Clerks* was playing in October, we were already in development on *Mallrats*."

Smith quickly and dramatically learned the value of making

a successful movie like *Clerks*: "What it did more than anything financially was to put me into the next inning of the ball game," he said. "Okay, here we go, now we're going to make a bigger movie."

Writer/director Steven Soderbergh ran into a similar situation after the release of what he felt would just be a resume piece: *sex, lies and videotape*. But he was also ready with a pocketful of ideas if opportunity came knocking—which it did, in spades.

Before his "little resume movie" had even hit Cannes, Soderbergh was approached to do another feature and had three projects set up quickly, all based on material he had loved for years: *The Last Ship* with Sydney Pollack at Universal … *King of the Hill*, another book, set up with Robert Redford … and *Kafka*, a script he had read previously and really loved. And despite the terrible odds in Hollywood, two of those projects actually got made.

"It's all very personal and a function of your character," Soderbergh explained. "I certainly had spent a lot of time thinking about what would happen if somebody came to me and said, 'What do you want to do next?' So, I had some answers.

"As my career has gone on, I've gotten more and more aggressive about keeping my plate full. I've got so many things that I want to do, so many ideas that I'd like to pursue, that it's hard to find time to do all of them. I'm mystified by directors who say, 'I can't find anything I want to do.' I look around and I want to do everything. There are stories everywhere.

"For those aspiring to a career in the film business, I offer this equation: Talent + Perseverance = Luck. Be ready when it happens."

The strategies that Smith, Soderbergh and others employed to anticipate and capitalize on their early success can be instructive for aspiring writers. While remaining focused on your current project, there are proactive steps you can take to be ready for any opportunities that arise:

- Maintaining an idea bank: This could mean keeping a document, notes app, or physical notebook filled with ideas. Record possible characters, settings, plot hooks, themes, or snippets of dialogue that catch your interest. Revisit this bank often for inspiration.
- Developing multiple projects: Some successful authors work on more than one novel or story collection at a time. This forces you to keep generating new writing and avoids the pressure of a single "make or break" project. The more practice you get, the better your chances of eventual success.
- Learning from other authors' examples: Studying how other writers successfully transitioned from one book to the next—what worked and what didn't—can provide valuable lessons for planning your own career trajectory. Find authors with a similar style or background to your own.

For an aspiring writer, the lesson from directors like Smith and Soderbergh is clear: always have more stories ready to tell. While focusing on your current work, fill your idea bank and network with potential supporters. Be ready the moment your career takes off, because when opportunity knocks, having your next project already in the works will ensure you hit the ground running.

Success breeds success.

. . .

BEYOND THE SCREEN QUESTIONS

- What concrete steps can you take to begin maintaining an idea bank of future projects? Start a document, notebook, or notes app and make it a habit to jot down ideas regularly.
- Are there any authors you could emulate in how they successfully transitioned from one hit book to the next? Study their strategies and lessons you could adopt for your own career.
- What's the next book you've always dreamed of writing? Treat your current project as a steppingstone to making that dream book a reality someday.
- What does "success breeds success" mean for your writing career? How could initial momentum propel you forward if you're prepared?
- What material do you already have that could form the basis of a future book? Revisit old characters, settings, plots, or themes you've explored in your writing thus far.

Film Suggestions

Clerks
Mallrats
sex, lies & videotape
King of the Hill
Kafka

PRINCIPLE #22

TAKE IT ALL WITH A GRAIN OF SALT

IMAGINE THIS: Your book is a monster hit. It tops all the best-seller lists. You end up on all the talk shows. Oprah has you over for tea. Offers are coming at you from all directions.

What do you do?

If you're smart, you take a deep breath and listen to the wise words of Dan Myrick.

Who—you ask—is Dan Myrick?

You may not know his name, but you know the name of a movie he co-directed: *The Blair Witch Project.*

While that was a classic horror film, the scarier story was what happened to his creative dreams <u>after</u> the movie became a huge success.

"Things changed dramatically," Myrick told me. "People all of a sudden want to do business with you and they want to make movies with you, and you didn't know them from Adam the day before. With that kind of notoriety, it's real easy to lose your perspective on this business and on this industry because of the success and how big it became. And it was good for us to remind each other where we were just a few months prior to *Blair Witch* hitting it big."

That's one of the downsides to sudden fame and success:

Everyone tells you that you're a big deal and the greatest thing since sliced bread. How do you respond? I think Myrick's choice was the wise one.

"You have to take it all with a grain of salt," Myrick said. "You really have to be happy and excited that you've reached the level of success that you've always dreamt about; but at the same time, remembering why you got into this business and remembering the kind of movies you wanted to make is very important as well. Because it's really easy to go down that road, where all of a sudden people are sending you scripts and they want to pay you a lot of money to do bad movies, just because they want to throw your name up on something.

"For me, it's about common sense," he continued. "We were offered several different movies, like *Exorcist 4.* I've forgotten the names of most of them. For better or worse—myself in particular—there's just a great reward in doing something that not everyone else is out doing. There's a certain level of freedom that keeping things in perspective can give you. You can go into a meeting and say "No" if you don't believe in the project.

"And I like having that freedom, I like having that autonomy."

BEYOND THE SCREEN QUESTIONS

- How does the story of Dan Myrick's experience with sudden fame and success resonate with your own aspirations as a novelist? What fears or potential pitfalls does it bring to mind?
- Myrick emphasizes the importance of remembering why you got into the business and the kind of movies (or in your case, novels) you wanted to make. How might this advice apply to your current writing project or career trajectory?

- What measures can you take now to ensure that you remember your original motivations and goals for your writing, even in the face of potential success and fame?
- Reflect on the idea of "taking it all with a grain of salt." How might this mindset influence your approach to both praise and criticism of your work?
- Myrick valued the freedom and autonomy to say "No" to projects that he didn't believe in. How can you practice this level of discernment in your own writing career, even before you achieve significant success?

Film Suggestions

Movies About Sudden Success

Amadeus
The Social Network
Almost Famous
La La Land
Fame

PRINCIPLE #23
NOBODY KNOWS ANYTHING

SCREENWRITER WILLIAM GOLDMAN SAID IT, and people in the film industry have been repeating it for years: NOBODY KNOWS ANYTHING.

Goldman knew a thing or two about how Hollywood operates. Besides his work as a novelist, he also penned screenplays for such films as *The Princess Bride*, *All The President's Men*, *Marathon Man*, *Misery*, and *Butch Cassidy and the Sundance Kid*, among others.

What does his classic phrase actually mean?

Here's how Goldman defined it: "Not one person in the entire motion picture field knows for a certainty what's going to work. Every time out it's a guess. And, if you're lucky, an educated one."

Some examples:

- The producers of the Julie Andrews flop, *Star!*, predicted the film to be a bigger hit than *The Sound of Music*. It wasn't. *The Sound of Music* had an initial theatrical release that lasted four and a half years, along with two successful re-releases. The film sold 283 million admissions worldwide and earned a total worldwide gross of $286 million. *Star!* cost about $14 million and ultimately made about $10 million worldwide.

- *Raiders of the Lost Ark* was turned down by all the major studios, despite the pedigree of its producer (George Lucas) and its director (Steven Spielberg). Paramount finally agreed to fund the film. It became one of the highest-grossing films of all time and was nominated for nine Academy Awards.
- Universal passed on *Star Wars.* It went on to gross $1 billion and spawned a franchise. Eventually, The Walt Disney Company purchased the Star Wars production company, Lucasfilm, for more than $4 billion.
- Columbia passed on *E.T. The Extra-Terrestrial.* If you adjust for inflation, the film went on to make about $1.3 billion.

How did any of this happen? Because nobody knows anything.

It's true in Hollywood. And it's just as true in the book world.

〠 〠 〠

"If I'm successful today, it's only because I know what worked yesterday."
　　—*Joe Calloway, Business Consultant*

This quote gets to the heart of William Goldman's famous phrase, "Nobody knows anything."

Even so-called experts are just piecing together past data and successes to make best guesses about the future. But ultimately, nobody can predict with certainty which stories will capture the hearts and imaginations of readers.

The examples Goldman shared in Hollywood illustrate this truth perfectly. Hit films succeeded not because studios accurately foresaw their potential, but in spite of the skepticism they initially faced.

The lesson for novelists is clear: don't worry too much about guessing what might sell. Instead, focus your energy on telling your story with honesty, passion and craftsmanship. Create the best novel you're capable of—one that stems from your unique voice, experiences and vision.

Stories that feel authentic and meaningful often transcend our attempts to strategize commercial "successes." So, as you write, set aside thoughts of the bestseller list. Sink into your story and characters, nurturing your own creative instincts. Trust that if you write from the heart, something true and beautiful will emerge.

Yesterday's successes came from creators focusing single-mindedly on their work, not the outcome.

So, tell your story, with honesty and conviction. You can't predict what might work tomorrow. But you can give every ounce of yourself to the act of creation today.

Like all great art, the rest will take care of itself.

BEYOND THE SCREEN QUESTIONS

- What major creative risks or unique ideas do you bring to your story that no one could have predicted will work? Lean into those instincts.
- How will you shield yourself from criticism and skepticism as you write the first draft? Remember, no one knows if this story will "work" yet—including you.
- Who is one writing partner you could share partial drafts with for support, without worrying about their opinions of its commercial potential?

- What mindset or daily mantra could you adopt to keep you focused solely on the process of writing, not the outcome? Repeat it to yourself often.
- What scene are you most excited to write—not because of its potential impact, but simply because you love the characters or setting involved? Start there to reignite your passion.

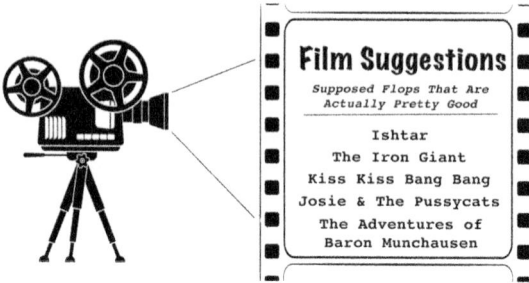

Film Suggestions

Supposed Flops That Are Actually Pretty Good

Ishtar

The Iron Giant

Kiss Kiss Bang Bang

Josie & The Pussycats

The Adventures of Baron Munchausen

AFTERWORD

Thank you for making it to the end of this book. I'm deeply grateful you took the time to read through all 23 principles and the stories of filmmakers that inspired them.

As you set out on your writing journey after reading this book, remember William Goldman's famous phrase: "Nobody knows anything."

Yes, you learned valuable principles from the filmmakers in these chapters. But ultimately, nobody—not agents, publishers, readers, or reviewers—can predict with certainty if your story will find an audience.

At its heart, this book highlights timeless lessons about craft, creativity, and the nature of storytelling. I hope you were able to identify principles that resonated with you personally and your own writing process. All the principles and stories shared in this book may not all fit your current needs, but that's okay. Your writing life is a moving river. Every time you step into that river, it's changed. Check back later and you may find gold which you missed the first time through.

The only thing that matters is sharing your unique voice and vision through the act of writing itself. So, as you begin your next novel, let go of expectations and give yourself permission to simply write the story that only you could tell.

Trust in your own writing voice and vision. There are no rules, only principles to guide and inspire you. With passion and perseverance, you'll find your way through the journey of writing a novel.

Thank you again for spending time with my book. I hope it has reminded you of your own potential as a novelist, and set you on a path of creativity, discovery, and joyful storytelling.

Now get writing!

John Gaspard
http://albertsbridgebooks.com

THE POPCORN PRINCIPLES

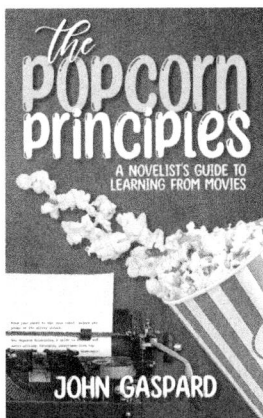

Take your novel to the next level.

Unlock the power of the silver screen with The Popcorn Principles, a guide to fiction and novel writing.

It will help you Craft unforgettable characters … Write compelling scenes … Hide exposition …Structure powerful endings

With this book (and the movies it draws on), you'll learn the tools and techniques used by screenwriters, which you can apply to your own writing.

Craft your next novel and become a better writer with The Popcorn Principles. (Popcorn not included.)

Grab it today!

https://www.albertsbridgebooks.com

GET YOUR FREE ELI MARKS SHORT STORY BUNDLE

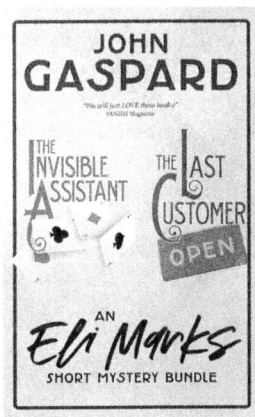

The Eli Marks Short Mystery Bundle
"The Invisible Assistant" & "The Last Customer"
Two short-story cozy mysteries in one!

"You will just LOVE these books." – VANISH Magazine

The Invisible Assistant

There's no question it was murder. But who killed whom?
What begins as a typical corporate event for magician Eli

Marks turns into a twisted mystery when he is called to the site of a recent murder/suicide. Confronted by the details of the grisly crime scene, Eli must sort through the post-mortem clues - and the bickering of the officials as well as a poorly-timed allergy attack - to determine just who murdered whom.

The Last Customer

The request was a first for Eli Marks: "Can you help me make my tuba disappear?"

Magician (and magic shop owner) Eli Marks is confronted with this odd demand just before he is about to close up shop for the day. Over the next few tense minutes, he finds a solution to that question which also, fortunately, puts him the positive side of what turns out to be a life-or-death situation.

Go to www.elimarksmysteries.com

GET YOUR FREE COMO LAKE PLAYERS SHORT MYSTERY

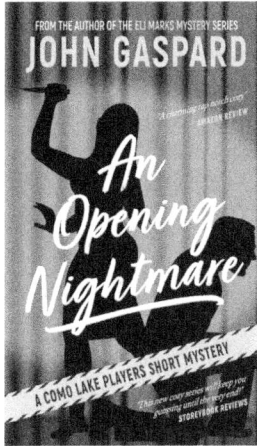

An Opening Nightmare

A Como Lake Players Short Mystery

A Killer Show, With the Corpses To Prove It

When an audience member is stabbed in the middle of an Opening Night performance, Leah must figure out who this clever killer is ... and make sure they don't kill the run of her show! Or murder her, as well!

A great introduction to The Como Lake Players mystery series: New Executive Director (and former actress) Leah Sexton must navigate the twisty world of community theater while dealing with crazy Board members, egomaniacal directors, self-centered actors ... and the occasional cold-blooded killer.

"This new cozy series will keep you guessing until the very end!" — Storeybook Reviews

Go to: https://www.albertsbridgebooks.com

JOIN THE NEWSLETTER

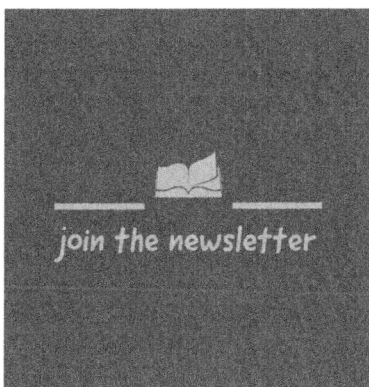

Keep in touch about all the books at Albert's Bridge books —
The Como Lake Players mysteries ... the Eli Marks mysteries ...
plus occasional deals on other mysteries, as well as film and
writing books! And no spam!

Go to: https://www.albertsbridgebooks.com

ABOUT THE AUTHOR

John is author of the Eli Marks mystery series as well as four other stand-alone novels, *"The Sword & Mr. Stone," "A Christmas Carl," "The Greyhound of the Baskervilles"* and *"The Ripperologists."*

He also writes the *Como Lake Players* mystery series.

In real life, John's not a magician, but he has directed six low-budget features that cost very little and made even less—that's no small trick.

He's also written books on the subject of low-budget film-making. Ironically, they've made more than the films. Those books (*"Fast, Cheap and Under Control"* and *"Fast, Cheap and Written That Way"*) are available in eBook, Paperback and audio-book formats.

John lives in Minnesota and shares his home with his lovely wife, several dogs, a few cats and a handful of pet allergies.

Find out more at: https://www.albertsbridgebooks.com and https://www.elimarksmysteries.com.

facebook.com/JohnGaspardAuthorPage
twitter.com/johngaspard
instagram.com/johngaspard
bookbub.com/authors/john-gaspard

BOOKS BY JOHN GASPARD

The Como Lake Players Mysteries
ACTING CAN BE MURDER
DYING TO AUDITION
REHEARSED TO DEATH
AN OPENING NIGHTMARE (Novella)

Stand-Alone Novels
THE SWORD & MR. STONE
A CHRISTMAS CARL
THE GREYHOUND OF THE BASKERVILLES
THE RIPPEROLOGISTS

NOTES

ALL THE QUOTES in the book—with the exception of the following citations—were taken from interviews conducted by the author for the books *Fast Cheap and Under Control, Fast Cheap and Written That Way, Tell Them It's a Dream Sequence, Women Make Movies* and The Fast, Cheap Movie Thoughts Blog.

Principle #1 - Beginning is Hard

"The scariest moment is always just before you start." King, Stephen, *On Writing*

"All good ideas start out as bad ideas…" Spielberg, Steven, https://industrialscripts.com/writing-process/

"A good writer is not someone who knows how to write …" Goldman, William, https://industrialscripts.com/writing-process/

"Screenwriting is like ironing…" Anderson, Paul Thomas, https://industrialscripts.com/writing-process/

"It's a simple thing he taught me…" Lynch, David, https://www.nytimes.com/1990/01/14/magazine/a-dark-lens-on-america.html

. . .

Principle #3 - Ignore the Voices in Your Head

"Writing is finally about one thing ..." Goldman, William, https://www.adazing.com/william-goldman-quotes-on-writing/

"I kept trying to push down the voice that was saying..." Hamm, Jon, https://thecreativemind.net/2666/quieting-our-inner-critic-for-more-creativity-and-confidence/

"No matter what you've done, there comes a point..." Hanks, Tom, https://www.npr.org/2016/08/29/491800907/tom-hanks-says-self-doubt-is-a-high-wire-act-that-we-all-walk

Principle #4 - Ignore the Voices <u>Outside</u> of Your Head

"We showed it to one guy..." Lynch, David, *Lynch on Lynch*

"For every film festival it got accepted to..." Lynch, David

"You Can't Hold Back the Human Spirit," www.wsws.org/art

Principle #5 - Unraveling the Thread of Theme

"No matter how silly a movie..." Howard, Ron, *Grand Theft Auto*, DVD Commentary

"So much of directing is managing your compromises..." Howard, Ron, *Grand Theft Auto*, DVD Commentary

"You start with your theme and your story..." Aronofsky, Darren, JaxomLOTUS, Interview with Darren Aronofsky, www.worth1000.com, October 19, 2000

"While working on this movie on paranoia..." Aronofsky, Darren, Darren Aronofsky: Easy as 3.14, www.combustiblecelluloid.com, June 1998

Principle #6 - Raise the Stakes

"True character is revealed in the choices a human being makes..." McKee, Robert, *Story: Substance, Structure, Style, and the Principles of Screenwriting*

"Be a sadist. No matter how sweet ..." Vonnegut, Kurt, https://www.writingclasses.com/toolbox/tips-masters/kurt-vonnegut-8-basics-of-creative-writing

Principle #12 - Take a Break
"Day off felt good. Saw Tucker: The Man and His Dream..." Soderbergh, Steven, *sex, lies and videotape Screenplay and Journal*, page 185

"I gave the editing crew the weekend off..." Aronofsky, Darren, *Pi, The Guerilla Diaries*, page 50

"Each person deserves a day..." Angelou, Maya, *Wouldn't Take Noting for My Journey Now*

"There is virtue in work and..." Cohen, Alan, *Wisdom of the Heart: Inspiration for a Life Worth Living*

Principle #13 - Concise Convos: The Art of Movie Dialogue
Scene from *Tootsie*: https://youtu.be/BnHqiipcw6g
Scene from *Big Night*: https://youtu.be/oerP7FRMWa8

Principle #15 - Play With Structure
"The modern writer must be an adventurer above all...", Quoted by Arthur Power in *Conversations with James Joyce*

Principle #19 - Rules Are Made To Be Broken
"The Lunch..." Demme, Jonathan, *AFI: The Directors*, DVD

Principle #21 - Anticipate Success
"We met (Hollywood producer) Jim Jacks..." Mosier, Scott, *An Askew View*, pages 62-63

"And I said, *Mallrats*..." Smith, Kevin, "Clerks Prove Ignorance is Bliss," *Moviemaker Magazine*, Issue No. 10, November 1994

"So, before Clerks ever came out..." Mosier, Scott, *An Askew View*, pages 62-63

"What it did more than anything financially..." Smith, Kevin, *Spike, Mike, Slackers & Dyke*s, page 233

"For those aspiring to a career in the film business..." Steven Soderbergh, Soderbergh, *Steven, sex, lies and videotape Screenplay and Journal*, page 7

Principle #23 - Nobody Knows Anything

"Nobody knows anything," Goldman, William, *Adventures in the Screen Trade*

"Not one person in the entire motion picture field ..." Goldman, William, *Adventures in the Screen Trade*

FILMOGRAPHY

FOR EASY REFERENCE, here are all the over 120 movies/TV shows mentioned throughout the book.

12 Monkeys
Screenwriters Janet Peoples, David Peoples
Dir. Terry Gilliam
Universal Pictures, 1995

2001: A Space Odyssey
Screenwriters Stanley Kubrick, Arthur C. Clarke
Dir. Stanley Kubrick
Metro-Goldwyn-Mayer (MGM), 1968

Adaptation
Screenwriters Charlie Kaufman, Donald Kaufman
Dir. Spike Jonze
Columbia Pictures, 2002

The Adventures of Baron Munchhausen
Screenwriter Terry Gilliam
Dir. Terry Gilliam
Columbia Pictures, 1988

Airplane!
Screenwriters Jim Abrahams, David Zucker, Jerry Zucker
Dir. Jim Abrahams, David Zucker, Jerry Zucker
Paramount Pictures, 1980

Almost Famous
Screenwriter Cameron Crowe
Dir. Cameron Crowe
DreamWorks Pictures, 2000

Amadeus
Screenwriter Peter Shaffer
Dir. Miloš Forman
Warner Bros. Pictures, 1984

Back to the Future
Screenwriters Robert Zemeckis, Bob Gale
Dir. Robert Zemeckis
Universal, 1985

Back to the Future 2
Screenwriter Bob Gale; Story by Zemeckis & Gale
Dir. Robert Zemeckis
Universal, 1989

Barton Fink
Screenwriters Ethan Coen, Joel Coen
Dir. Joel Coen
20th Century Fox, 1991

A Beautiful Mind
Screenwriter Akiva Goldsman
Dir. Ron Howard
Universal Pictures, 2001

Before the Devil Knows You're Dead
Screenwriter Kelly Masterson
Dir. Sidney Lumet
The Weinstein Company, 2007

Being John Malkovich
Screenwriter Charlie Kaufman
Dir. Spike Jonze
Gramercy Pictures, 1999

Best in Show
Screenwriters Christopher Guest, Eugene Levy
Dir. Christopher Guest
USA Films, 2000

The Big Lebowski
Screenwriters Ethan Coen, Joel Coen
Dir. Joel Coen, Ethan Coen
Gramercy Pictures, 1998

Caged Heat
Screenwriters Jonathan Demme, Tracy Torme
Dir. Jonathan Demme
New World Pictures, 1974

Can You Ever Forgive Me
Screenwriter Nicole Holofcener
Dir. Marielle Heller
Searchlight Pictures, 2018

Capote
Screenwriter Dan Futterman
Dir. Bennett Miller
MGM Studios, 2005

Casablanca
Screenwriters Julius J. Epstein,
Philip G. Epstein, Howard Koch
Dir. Michael Curtiz
Warner Bros., 1942

Citizen Kane
Screenwriters Orson Welles, Herman J. Mankiewicz
Dir. Orson Welles
RKO Radio Pictures, 1941

Clerks
Screenwriter Kevin Smith
Dir. Kevin Smith
Miramax, 1994

A Clockwork Orange
Screenwriter Anthony Burgess
Dir. Stanley Kubrick
Warner Bros., 1971

The Dark Knight
Screenwriters Jonathan Nolan, Christopher Nolan
Dir. Christopher Nolan
Warner Bros. Pictures, 2008

The Empire Strikes Back
Screenwriters Lawrence Kasdan, Leigh Brackett
Dir. Irvin Kershner
Lucasfilm, 1980

Face/Off
Screenwriters Mike Werb, Michael Colleary
Dir. John Woo
Paramount Pictures, 1997

Fail-Safe
Screenwriters Walter Bernstein,
Eugene Burdick, Harvey Wheeler
Dir. Sidney Lumet
Columbia Pictures, 1964

Fame
Screenwriter Christopher Gore
Dir. Alan Parker
MGM, 1980

Fatal Attraction
Screenwriter James Dearden
Dir. Adrian Lyne
Paramount Pictures, 1987

Ferris Bueller's Day Off
Screenwriter John Hughes
Dir. John Hughes
Paramount Pictures, 1986

Field of Dreams
Screenwriter Phil Alden Robinson
Dir. Phil Alden Robinson
Universal Pictures, 1989

Fight Club
Screenwriters Chuck Palahniuk, Jim Uhls
Dir. David Fincher
20th Century Fox, 1999

The Four Musketeers
Screenwriter George MacDonald Fraser
Dir. Richard Lester
The Ladd Company, 1974

Frida
Screenwriter Diane Lake
Dir. Julie Taymor
Miramax Films, 2002

Get Out
Screenwriter Jordan Peele
Dir. Jordan Peele
Universal Pictures, 2017

The Godfather
Screenwriters Mario Puzo, Francis Ford Coppola
Dir. Francis Ford Coppola
Paramount Pictures, 1972

Goodfellas
Screenwriters Nicholas Pileggi, Martin Scorsese
Dir. Martin Scorsese
Warner Bros., 1990

The Great British Bake Off
Creator Love Productions BBC, 2010

Groundhog Day
Screenwriters Danny Rubin, Harold Ramis
Dir. Harold Ramis
Columbia Pictures, 1993

Halloween
Screenwriters John Carpenter, Debra Hill
Dir. John Carpenter
Compass International Pictures, 1978

Heaven's Gate
Screenwriter Michael Cimino
Dir. Michael Cimino
United Artists, 1980

High Noon
Screenwriter Carl Foreman
Dir. Fred Zinnemann
Stanley Kramer Productions, 1952

Identity
Screenwriter Michael Cooney
Dir. James Mangold
Capella International, 2003

Inception
Screenwriter Christopher Nolan
Dir. Christopher Nolan
Warner Bros., 2010

The Iron Giant
Screenwriters Brad Bird, Tim McCanlies
Dir. Brad Bird
Warner Bros. Animation, 1999

Ishtar
Screenwriter Elaine May
Dir. Elaine May
Columbia Pictures, 1987

The Italian Job
Screenwriter Troy Kennedy-Martin
Dir. Peter Collinson
Paramount Pictures, 1969

It's a Wonderful Life
Screenwriters Frances Goodrich,
Albert Hackett, Frank Capra, Jo Swerling
Dir. Frank Capra
Liberty Films, 1946

Jaws
Screenwriters Peter Benchley,
Carl Gottlieb, Howard Sackler
Dir. Steven Spielberg
Universal Pictures, 1975

Josie and the Pussycats
Screenwriters Harry Elfont,
Deborah Kaplan, Dan Crawford
Dir. Harry Elfont and Deborah Kaplan
Universal Pictures, 2001

Judy Berlin
Screenwriter Eric Mendelsohn
Dir. Eric Mendelsohn
Image Entertainment, 1999

Kafka
Screenwriter Lem Dobbs
Dir. Steven Soderbergh
Gramercy Pictures, 1991

King of the Hill
Screenwriter Steven Soderbergh
Dir. Steven Soderbergh
Gramercy Pictures, 1993

Kiss Kiss Bang Bang
Screenwriter Shane Black
Dir. Shane Black
Lions Gate Films, 2005

La La Land
Screenwriters Damien Chazelle, Justin Hurwitz
Dir. Damien Chazelle
Summit Entertainment, 2016

Lars and the Real Girl
Screenwriter Nancy Oliver
Dir. Craig Gillespie
MGM, 2007

The Last Broadcast
Screenwriters Stefan Avalos, Lance Weiler
Dir. Stefan Avalos, Lance Weiler
101 Films, 1998

The LEGO Movie
Screenwriters Phil Lord, Christopher Miller
Dir. Phil Lord and Christopher Miller
Warner Bros., 2014

Limitless
Screenwriter Leslie Dixon
Dir. Neil Burger
Relativity Media, 2011

Lincoln
Screenwriter Tony Kushner
Dir. Steven Spielberg
DreamWorks Pictures, 2012

Little Miss Sunshine
Screenwriters Michael Arndt, Jonathan Dayton, Valerie Faris
Dirs. Jonathan Dayton and Valerie Faris
Fox Searchlight Pictures, 2006

Living in Oblivion
Screenwriter Tom DiCillo
Dir. Tom DiCillo
Columbia TriStar Home Video, 1995

The Lord of the Rings: The Return of the King
Screenwriters Fran Walsh, Philippa Boyens,
Peter Jackson, J.R.R. Tolkien (novel)
Dir. Peter Jackson
New Line Cinema, 2003

Magnolia
Screenwriter Paul Thomas Anderson
Dir. Paul Thomas Anderson
New Line Cinema, 1999

Mallrats
Screenwriter Kevin Smith
Dir. Kevin Smith
View Askew Productions, 1995

Man on the Moon
Screenwriters Scott Alexander, Larry Karaszewski
Dir. Milos Forman
Universal Pictures, 1999

Marley & Me
Screenwriter David Annenberg
Dir. David Frankel
20th Century Fox, 2008

Memento
Screenwriter Christopher Nolan
Dir. Christopher Nolan
Newmarket Films, 2000

Modern Times
Screenwriter Charlie Chaplin
Dir. Charlie Chaplin
United Artists, 1936

Moonrise Kingdom
Screenwriters Wes Anderson, Roman Coppola
Dir. Wes Anderson
Indian Paintbrush, 2012

Mulholland Drive
Screenwriter David Lynch
Dir. David Lynch
Universal Pictures, 2001

The Muppet Show (TV series)
Creator Jim Henson
ITC Entertainment, 1976

Napoleon Dynamite
Screenwriter Jared Hess
Dir. Jared Hess
Fox Searchlight Pictures, 2004

No Country for Old Men
Screenwriters Ethan Coen, Joel Coen
Dir. Ethan Coen and Joel Coen
Paramount Vantage, 2007

Once Upon a Time in Hollywood
Screenwriter Quentin Tarantino
Dir. Quentin Tarantino
Sony Pictures, 2019

On the Waterfront
Screenwriter Budd Schulberg
Dir. Elia Kazan
Horizon Pictures, 1954

Personal Velocity: Three Portraits
Screenwriter Rebecca Miller
Dir. Rebecca Miller
United Artists, 2002

The Philadelphia Story
Screenwriters Donald Ogden Stewart, Philip Barry
Dir. George Cukor
Metro-Goldwyn-Mayer (MGM), 1940

pi
Screenwriters Darren Aronofsky,
Sean Gullette, Eric Watson
Dir. Darren Aronofsky
Harvest Filmworks, 1998

Psycho
Screenwriter Joseph Stefano
Dir. Alfred Hitchcock
Shamley Productions, 1960

Pulp Fiction
Screenwriter Quentin Tarantino
Dir. Quentin Tarantino
Miramax Films, 1994

Raiders of the Lost Ark
Screenwriters George Lucas,
Philip Kaufman, Lawrence Kasdan
Dir. Steven Spielberg
Lucasfilm, 1981

Ratatouille
Screenwriters Brad Bird, Jan Pinkava,
Jim Capobianco, Thomas McCarthy, Emran Mian
Dir. Brad Bird / Jan Pinkava
Walt Disney Pictures, 2007

Re-Animator
Screenwriters Stuart Gordon,
William J. Norris, Dennis Paoli
Dir. Stuart Gordon
Empire Pictures, 1985

Rocky
Screenwriter Sylvester Stallone
Dir. John G. Avildsen
United Artists, 1976

Roger Dodger
Screenwriter Dylan Kidd
Dir. Dylan Kidd
Strand Releasing, 2002

Run Lola Run
Screenwriter Tom Tykwer
Dir. Tom Tykwer
X-Filme Creative Pool, 1998

Scream
Screenwriter Kevin Williamson
Dir. Wes Craven
Dimension Films, 1996

Selma
Screenwriter Paul Webb
Dir. Ava DuVernay
Paramount Pictures, 2014

sex, lies and videotape
Screenwriter Steven Soderbergh
Dir. Steven Soderbergh
RCA / Columbia Pictures Home Video, 1989

Shaun of the Dead
Screenwriters Simon Pegg, Edgar Wright
Dir. Edgar Wright
StudioCanal, 2004

Schindler's List
Screenwriter Steven Zaillian
Dir. Steven Spielberg
Universal Pictures, 1993

The Shining
Screenwriter Stanley Kubrick
Dir. Stanley Kubrick
Warner Bros., 1980

Shutter Island
Screenwriters Laeta Kalogridis, Dennis Lehane (novel)
Dir. Martin Scorsese
Paramount Pictures, 2010

The Silence of the Lambs
Screenwriter Ted Tally
Dir. Jonathan Demme
Orion Pictures, 1991

Silent Movie
Screenwriters Mel Brooks, Ron Clark,
Rudy De Luca, Barry Levinson
Dir. Mel Brooks
Associated Film Distribution, 1976

The Sixth Sense
Screenwriter M. Night Shyamalan
Dir. M. Night Shyamalan
Hollywood Pictures, 1999

Sliding Doors
Screenwriter Peter Howitt
Dir. Peter Howitt
Miramax Films, 1998

The Social Network
Screenwriter Aaron Sorkin
Dir. David Fincher
Columbia Pictures, 2010

Someone To Love
Screenwriter Henry Jaglom
Dir. Henry Jaglom
Jaglom Productions, 1987

The Sound of Music
Screenwriters Ernest Lehman,
Howard Lindsay, Russel Crouse
Dir. Robert Wise
20th Century Fox, 1965

Speed
Screenwriter Graham Yost
Dir. Jan de Bont
20th Century Fox, 1994

Splash
Screenwriters Lowell Ganz, Babaloo Mandel
Dir. Ron Howard
Touchstone Pictures, 1984

Star!
Screenwriter William Robert Wells
Dir. Robert Wise
20th Century Fox, 1968

Star Wars: Episode IV - A New Hope
Screenwriter George Lucas
Dir. George Lucas
Lucasfilm, 1977

Steel Magnolias
Screenwriter Robert Harling
Dir. Herbert Ross
TriStar Pictures, 1989

subUrbia
Screenwriter Eric Bogosian
Dir. Richard Linklater
October Films, 1996

Suckers
Screenwriters Roger Nygard, Joe Yanetty
Dir. Roger Nygard
Blink., 1999

Sunset Boulevard
Screenwriters Charles Brackett, Billy Wilder, D.M. Marshman Jr.
Dir. Billy Wilder
Paramount Pictures, 1950

Taken
Screenwriters Luc Besson, Robert Mark Kamen
Dir. Pierre Morel
EuropaCorp, 2008

Targets
Screenwriter Peter Bogdanovich
Dir. Peter Bogdanovich
Roger Corman Productions, 1968

Terminator 2: Judgment Day
Screenwriters James Cameron, William Wisher
Dir. James Cameron
TriStar Pictures, 1991

The Thing
Screenwriter Bill Lancaster
Dir. John Carpenter
Universal Pictures, 1982

The Three Musketeers
Screenwriter George MacDonald Fraser
Dir. Richard Lester
The Ladd Company, 1973

Titanic
Screenwriter James Cameron
Dir. James Cameron
20th Century Fox, 1997

Tootsie
Screenwriters Larry Gelbart,
Murray Schisgal, Don McGuire
Dir. Sydney Pollack
Columbia Pictures, 1982

Toy Story
Screenwriters John Lasseter,
Andrew Stanton, Joel Cohen, Alec Sokolow
Dir. John Lasseter
Pixar Animation Studios, 1995

Toy Story 3
Screenwriters Michael Arndt,
Lee Unkrich, Andrew Stanton, John Lasseter
Dir. Lee Unkrich
Walt Disney Pictures, 2010

Tucker: The Man and His Dream
Screenwriter David S. Ward
Dir. Francis Ford Coppola
Paramount Pictures, 1988

Twin Peaks (TV series)
Creators David Lynch, Mark Frost
Lynch/Frost Productions, 1990

The Usual Suspects
Screenwriter Christopher McQuarrie
Dir. Bryan Singer
Bryan Singer Productions, 1995

Up
Screenwriters Pete Docter,
Bob Peterson, Tom McCarthy
Dir. Pete Docter
Pixar Animation Studios, 2009

Vertigo
Screenwriters Alec Coppel, Samuel Taylor
Dir. Alfred Hitchcock
Alfred J. Hitchcock Productions, 1958

Walk the Line
Screenwriter Gill Dennis, James Mangold
Dir. James Mangold
20th Century Fox, 2005

Waking Life
Screenwriter Richard Linklater
Dir. Richard Linklater
Fox Searchlight Pictures, 2001

Wargames
Screenwriters Lawrence Lasker, Walter F. Parkes
Dir. John Badham
The Herald Company, 1983

Waterworld
Screenwriters Peter Rader, David Twohy
Dir. Kevin Reynolds
Universal Pictures, 1995

What Happened Was ...
Screenwriter Tom Noonan
Dir. Tom Noonan
Genre Pictures, 1994

World War Z
Screenwriters Matthew Michael Carnahan,
Drew Goddard, Damon Lindelof
Dir. Marc Forster
Paramount Pictures, 2013

Worst Week of My Life (TV Series)
Creators: Nick Abbott and Paul Duddridge
BBC, 2004

X-Men: The Last Stand
Screenwriters Simon Kinberg, Zak Penn
Dir. Brett Ratner
20th Century Fox, 2006

Printed in Great Britain
by Amazon

26788270R00086